BEDTIME STORIES FOR WORRIED LIBERALS

STUART HERITAGE is a writer and columnist for *The Times*, *Guardian*, *i* and *Esquire*, and the author of *Don't be a Dick, Pete*. In addition to this, he has written for a range of publications and television programmes, founded and edited award-winning blogs. For two years running he was named as one of the fifty most influential emerging figures in the British media by the *Independent*, an honour that has singularly failed to manifest itself into anything even slightly meaningful. He is going bald.

BEDTIME STORIES

FOR

WORRIED

LIBERALS

Stuart Heritage

P

PROFILE BOOKS

This paperback edition published in 2020

First published in Great Britain in 2019 by
Profile Books Ltd
29 Cloth Fair
London ECIA 7JQ

www.profilebooks.com

Typeset in Dante by MacGuru Ltd
Printed and bound in Great Britain by
Clays Ltd, Elcograf S.p.A.

A CIP catalogue record for this book is
available from the British Library.

ISBN 978 1 78816 338 5
eISBN 978 1 78283 606 3

MIX
Paper | Supporting
responsible forestry
FSC® C018072
FSC
www.fsc.org

For Dad

Contents

Prologue

Hello. My name is Stuart, and I'm here to tell you some bedtime stories.

It has been a long and tiring day, hasn't it? Just like every other day, it's been full of fear and anger and microaggressions by the bucketload. The world is teetering on the edge of political, environmental and nuclear destruction, and every day it seems to get a little bit worse. Sometimes it feels like the bullies have won.

But between the covers of this book you will find some respite. In this selection of soothing fantasy stories, our opponents get to learn the error of their ways: politicians atone, demagogues are called out, and Boris Johnson gets mauled to death by bears. The message that runs through every page here is simple: *Everything is going to be fine*.

So snuggle up, snowflakes, and close your eyes.

Tomorrow will be just as difficult as today but, right now, there's nothing to trigger you. This book is your safe space and you, dear reader, are safe here.

Camerella

Once upon a time, big news came to town. The king was to hold a ball, the biggest ball in the land, full of dancing and merriment. It was to be called The Wilderness Festival, and it was to be headlined by Groove Armada. Everyone was invited.

Well, everyone except for David Cameron. He longed to attend the ball, but his wicked stepmother always refused, telling him that he couldn't go anywhere until he'd cleaned up all the mess. So instead he passed his days glumly staring through the window of his £25,000 shepherd's hut and dreaming of what could have been. Oh, the things he'd do if he ever got to visit the Wilderness Festival. He'd drink beer. He'd smoke cigarettes. He'd dress up in a nice anorak and just sort of wander around the place weighed down by a cloak of pure sadness.

But instead he had to stay in his hut. When the

day of the ball came, David Cameron watched as his wicked stepmother, his wicked stepsisters and his wife Samantha all laced up their most beautiful frocks, put on their Barbour jackets and set off to the festival in a fleet of golden coaches.

'Goodbye!' he called out to them. 'Have a wonderful time!' But nobody replied, except for his stepmother, who simply shouted 'Clean up all the mess!'

David Cameron slumped down in his chair, surrounded by Post-It notes covered with rejected titles for his memoir, including *This Wasn't My Fault* and *I Just Want To Go Outside Again*, and he sighed. 'I wish I could go to the Wilderness Festival too.'

And then – boomf – a fairy godmother appeared before him in a puff of smoke.

'You called?' said the fairy godmother.

'I don't think I did,' replied David Cameron. 'Who are you?'

'Why, your fairy godmother, of course,' she answered. 'I have come to grant your one true wish! By the way, nice shed you've got here.'

'It's actually a shepherd's hut,' replied David Cameron. 'But thank you. I sort of wish it hadn't come to single-handedly represent the gilded isolation that I forced upon myself the moment I called the referendum all those years ago, but I suppose beggars can't be choosers, ha ha.'

The fairy godmother had never heard a laugh quite like it in all of her days. It sounded incredibly sad, like a collapsed circus tent. So disturbed was she, in fact, that she instantly tried to change the subject.

'What colour is this, anyway?' she asked, gesturing vaguely at the walls.

'Clunch', repeated David Cameron. "It's a Farrow and Ball shade. You can look it up online and everything'.

'I beg your pardon?' asked the fairy godmother.

'Clunch,' repeated David Cameron. 'It's a Farrow and Ball shade.'

'Weird,' said the fairy godmother. 'But now you must tell me the wish you would like to be granted.'

David Cameron gulped. This was really going to be it. This was the moment where he would finally be given everything he ever wanted.

'I wish to go to the Wilderness Festival,' he smiled.

The fairy godmother looked confused. 'Sorry, what?' she stammered.

'The Wilderness Festival,' he replied. 'I would like one ticket to the Wilderness Festival please.'

'That's your wish?'

'Yes, that's my wish.'

'Not going back in time and reversing your decision to call the referendum?'

David Cameron stopped dead in his tracks. He

hadn't thought of that. Perhaps she had a point. Perhaps he could choose to go back in time and take a harder line against the Eurosceptic wing of the Conservative Party, preventing the referendum and the Brexit chaos and Britain's slow slide towards irreparable international irrelevance.

'Nah,' he said after a pause. 'One ticket to Wilderness please.'

The fairy godmother was furious. The whole reason she had visited David Cameron in the first place was to offer him one last shot at redeeming his tattered reputation. But no, here he was, spunking it all away on a ticket to watch Tom Odell perform to a crowd of disinterested toffs. She couldn't let him blow his big chance like this. She had to think of something to salvage this mess.

'Let's put it to a vote,' she said.

'A what?' whispered David Cameron, suddenly terrified.

'A vote!' said the fairy godmother. 'What a brilliant idea!'

So the fairy godmother invited one hundred of her fairy godmother friends to the hut, so that she and Cameron could argue their respective cases to them – remain in the shed or leave for the festival – before the godmothers had a decisive say in the matter.

One by one the fairy godmothers boomf-ed into

view, and David Cameron went first. He argued that Wilderness would let him indulge all his favourite hobbies, like smoking cigarettes and drinking lager and taking slightly shamefaced ironic selfies with people who openly disliked him. He made beer mats extolling the benefits of Wilderness. He invented wild promises and painted them on the side of a bus. When he finished, an uneasy silence fell over the group.

Then it was the fairy godmother's turn. She put much less effort into her argument, because she was arguing to a group of other fairy godmothers, and surely none of them would be stupid enough to buy any of Cameron's crap.

Then came the vote. The fairy godmothers huddled together for a few minutes, before the leader stepped forward.

'The fairy godmothers have made their decision,' she stated. 'We vote forty-eight in favour of time travel, and fifty-two in favour of Wilderness.'

'Score!' said David Cameron, pumping his arm like a stockbroker on a tennis court.

'Hold on, hold on,' spluttered the fairy godmother. 'Are you sure you all fully understood the conse- quences of the vote?'

'Yes, they're sure,' crowed David Cameron. 'Now give me my ticket.'

The fairy godmother thought about this for a

moment, and then made the only logical decision available to her.

'I quit,' she said.

David Cameron was appalled. 'You can't quit! Not without delivering me my ticket! This whole vote was your idea! Just because you failed to take the electorate seriously during your campaign, it doesn't mean you get to swan off scot-free and leave everyone else to clean up your … ah, no, OK, I see what's going on now. OK, that's fair enough.'

And just like that – boomf! – the fairy godmother vanished in another puff of smoke.

David Cameron looked at the fifty-two fairy godmothers who'd voted his way. A flicker of hope flashed across his eyes. 'Which of you will deliver your promise to send me to Wilderness?' he asked.

From the back of the group, two fairy godmothers pushed their way forwards. It was Theresa May and David Davis.

'We will!' they cried.

'Oh fuck,' muttered David Cameron.

The Faceflautist of Hamelin

Once upon a time, the town of Hamelin was overrun with trouble. Hidden among the town were countless racists and bigots and liars, but nobody knew who they were. The residents of the town were beside themselves with worry, scared that they might live with a secret fascist, and the mayor was at a loss.

'If only there was some way to weed out this unsavoury element,' he cried. But there wasn't.

To be sure, the mayor had tried everything he could think of. He'd tried asking the townspeople who among them were racist, but this only angered the good-hearted majority. He'd attempted to build a private education centre, to try to dissuade the secret bigots against their prejudices, but this also failed.

Threats didn't work. Bribery didn't work. The mayor didn't know what to do.

And then one day, a strange-looking man came to town with great noise and bluster. 'Did I hear somebody mention undetected racists?' he asked the mayor.

The mayor looked upon this strange man, with his abnormally large head, unfeasibly boring grey T-shirt and his general air of never having met or spoken to any real human being before, and he was curious. 'What's it to you, stranger?' he asked the man. 'Who are you?'

'My name is Mark Zuckerberg,' said the man, 'And I have invented a solution to all your problems.'

The man unzipped his bag and pulled out a long metal pipe. 'Behold!' he cried. 'This is the Faceflute! When I start playing this miraculous instrument, the worst people who live in this town will be helpless against its melody. They'll show themselves for who they truly are once they succumb to the magic of my amazing Faceflute.'

The mayor was still suspicious. 'Stranger, this Faceflute sounds amazing indeed,' he said. 'But we are a poor town, and we have no money with which to pay you.'

'I bring good news!' said the stranger. 'My Faceflute is free! All I ask is that, in return for my services, everyone in this town writes down and gives me their name, their gender, their birthday, their email address and six to ten of their main interests.'

Again, the mayor was unsure. 'But stranger,' he cried, 'we value our privacy here, and the thought of divulging such information to an outsider makes us uneasy.'

'Don't be like that,' said the stranger. 'Look at this face. Does this look like the face of someone you can't trust?'

'No,' said the mayor, leaving unspoken the fact that it actually looked like the face of an android that had been struck by lightning and was starting to malfunction.

'Great!' said the stranger. 'Then I'll begin.'

And so the stranger walked through the streets, playing an eerie melody on his flute. And as he passed each window, every secret bigot in the town found themselves helpless against its power. The moment they heard its music, they came rushing out of their front doors, blurting out whatever intolerable rubbish they'd been trying to hide so desperately.

'This country is full!' shouted one man, as he chased after the stranger.

'I'm not being funny, but why is there a mosque here?' shouted another.

The stranger wound his way across the town, along every lane and avenue.

'U LOST GET OVER IT!' shouted a woman as she joined the throng.

'I DRESSED UP AS A GOLLIWOG WHEN I WAS A LITTLE GIRL AND I THINK THE FACT THAT NOBODY DOES THIS ANY MORE IS THE REASON

WHY THIS ENTIRE COUNTRY HAS GONE DOWN THE DRAIN!' shouted another.

'MAKE AMERICA GREAT AGAIN!' shouted a third.

Soon the Faceflute had tricked every awful resident of the town into screaming their most inappropriate thoughts into the air. A huge angry crowd formed, each member following the stranger and muttering about Enoch Powell having a point.

The stranger led the crowd to a cave and kept playing as, one after another, the bigots walked inside of their own accord. Once the last of them was safely in, the stranger stopped playing and rolled a large boulder over the entrance. The town was finally free of trouble.

The mayor was overjoyed. 'Thank you, thank you!' he cried to the stranger. 'Your Faceflute is indeed a miracle. Now, finally, this is once again a town to be proud of.'

'It was no problem,' said the stranger. 'Now, all I ask in return are the details you promised.'

'Erm, yes, about that,' stammered the mayor. 'We've been having a bit of a think about this, and actually we aren't all that comfortable just handing over such personal information.'

The stranger was angry. 'Then the price just went up,' he growled. 'Now I want everyone's name, gender, birthday, email address, interests *and* a constantly updated list of everything they have ever physically looked at.'

'But that's insane!' pleaded the mayor. 'Nobody in their right mind would ever agree to ...'

'Everyone else already has!' shouted the stranger. 'And now, for defying me, you shall pay a heavy price! A heavy price INDEED!'

So the stranger took out his Faceflute once more and began to play. This time the tune he played was slow and sinister.

'I don't see what the point of this is,' said the mayor. 'You've already rid us of our racists, so what more can ...'

And, just like that, the Faceflute destroyed the town's newspaper industry.

'Stop! Stop!' the mayor cried.

But the stranger wouldn't stop. He kept playing until the town's classified ad and greetings card industries had also been decimated.

'Please! Enough! I beg of you!' the mayor cried.

But the stranger didn't listen. He kept playing until everyone in the town started experiencing low-level anxiety about how their friends and relatives appeared to lead happier and more exciting lives than they did.

'We thought your flute was created for good!' wept the mayor. 'But now we can see that it is an instrument of pure evil.'

But the stranger kept playing. He played so hard

that he created a hyper-personalised newsfeed for each resident that secretly reinforced their existing opinions and removed all opposing viewpoints, until all sensible middle-ground consensus had been obliterated, leaving just two permanently warring fringes. The mayor was sacked. Donald Trump was voted in as his replacement. It was a disaster.

But then something magical happened. One by one, each entirely of their own accord, the townspeople started to break free of the Faceflute's magic. Nothing huge happened. Nobody died. Everyone just started getting bored with Faceflute as an idea, just as they'd previously got bored with MyFlute and Flutester and Flutes Reunited.

Before long, the stranger's power over the town had almost completely diminished. As he ran away in defeat, the townspeople once again started to see each other for who they really were: flesh-and-blood people rather than a bundle of exaggerated digital opinions. Bonds grew. Old battle lines disintegrated. Little by little, Hamelin became a town once more.

Three months later, a new stranger came to town. 'Hi!' he shouted. 'My name's @Jack and I'm here to demonstrate the amazing power of my Twitter Kazoo! Why, just one blow and …'

So the townspeople tied him up and threw him in a lake, and they all lived happily ever after.

Bojolocks and The Three Bears

Once upon a time, in a cottage in the forest, lived three bears: a Daddy Bear, a Mummy Bear and a Baby Bear. One morning, Mummy Bear made porridge for her family and served it up in three bowls. But the porridge was too hot, so the three bears went out for a walk while it cooled down.

After a few hours, the bears returned home and noticed that their front door was ajar. 'That's funny,' thought Mummy Bear, 'I could have sworn that I locked it when we left.'

The bears sat down in the kitchen to eat their porridge. Daddy Bear looked down at his bowl with a scowl. 'Someone's been eating my porridge,' he growled.

Mummy Bear looked down at her bowl, too. 'Someone's been eating MY porridge,' she growled.

So Baby Bear looked down at his bowl as well. 'Someone's been eating my porridge, and they've eaten it all up!' he cried.

Upset, the three bears walked into their living room, and made another unpleasant discovery. 'Someone's been sitting in my chair,' grumbled Daddy Bear.

'Someone's been sitting in MY chair,' grumbled Mummy Bear.

Baby Bear looked down at a pile of tattered wood. 'Someone's been sitting in my chair, and they've broken it into splinters,' he sobbed.

Daddy Bear snarled a toothy snarl. 'I think we have an intruder in our house,' he snarled. 'My guess is that they're probably fast asleep in one of our beds at the moment, so we need to very carefully and very quietly sneak upstairs to …'

Just then, a large startled creature barrelled down the stairs. It was a strange creature indeed, one that looked like a puppet taped together from bits of abandoned sofa, topped with a strange blond wig.

The creature rounded the corner at the foot of the stairs and ploughed straight into Baby Bear, knocking him straight to the ground. 'Hey! Don't do that!' cried Baby Bear, 'I'm just a kid.'

'Sorry old bean,' garbled the creature in the manner of a toad submerged in Pimms, 'Force of habit, I'm afraid.'

Daddy Bear was furious. 'Who the hell do you think you are?'

'Why, I'm very obviously Boris Johnson', replied the creature. 'I thought you'd have figured that out by now.'

'You ate all our porridge!' shouted Mummy Bear, accusingly.

'Ah, yes, porridge' harrumphed Boris Johnson. 'Splendid British culinary invention. A full fat, fast out of the blocks, full-fibre broadband, should-have-gone-to-Specsavers triumph of a breakfast. In fact, I believe it was Winston Churchill who once said that porridge …'

As Boris Johnson continued to extol the virtues of porridge in the form of a ramshackle, apparently off-the-cuff speech, Baby Bear turned to his parents and said, 'He's using all these words, but he isn't actually saying anything.'

Daddy Bear looked down and saw the confusion in his son's eyes. 'Don't worry boy, I've got this,' he growled, before charging at Boris Johnson and pinning him to the wall.

'WHY DID YOU EAT OUR PORRIDGE?' he roared.

'Porridge? What? Me? No, no, old chap, you must be mistaken. Rotten stuff. I never touch it,' stammered Boris Johnson.

'You just called it a triumph,' yelled Mummy Bear.

'Yes, I did, didn't I?' admitted Boris Johnson.

'So which one is true?' asked Baby Bear. 'Do you think that porridge is rotten or a triumph? Which one do you really believe?'

'That depends. Which one is going to get me out of trouble the fastest?' asked Boris Johnson.

'This guy has absolutely no courage in his convictions whatsoever,' whispered Baby Bear to his mother.

'I don't know,' replied Mummy Bear. 'He's sort of charming.'

Daddy Bear didn't like Boris Johnson's answer. As calmly as he could, with Boris still pinned to the wall, he explained that he was a reasonable and tolerant bear. As such, he'd give Boris Johnson ten seconds to get out of their house.

'Listen,' began Boris Johnson, 'Before I go, I really ought to walk you through some of the other changes I made in your absence. It'll only take a hot second, as the kids say these days.'

'Changes?' growled Daddy Bear. 'What changes?'

Boris Johnson gulped. 'Well, I've exchanged your car for a newer model,' he stammered.

'You've done WHAT?' roared Daddy Bear.

Boris explained that, while there was nothing technically wrong with the bears' old car – in fact, some regarded it as something of a design classic – it didn't really meet the demands of modern-day forests. 'And so I've given you *this*,' said Boris Johnson, pointing out of the house at something that, at first glance, looked exactly like the old car, except with a weird diagonal window. 'Isn't she a beauty?'

'How does that window open?' asked Mummy Bear.

'It doesn't,' replied Boris Johnson.

'So there's air-con?' asked Mummy Bear.

'Not really,' replied Boris Johnson.

'So what do we do on a hot day?' asked Mummy Bear.

'Boil to death inside your own skin, I suppose!', replied Boris Johnson. Then, sensing dissatisfaction, he added 'Ah, I've also bought you a new front door.'

'You've replaced our front door?' asked Baby Bear.

'No, that's not what I said,' replied Boris Johnson. 'This is a wonderful, entirely new, supplemental front door designed to sit next to your existing door,' he said.

'But we only need one door,' said Daddy Bear.

Boris Johnson was undaunted. 'But this is a garden door,' he argued. 'It's beautiful. Joanna Lumley suggested it to me. You'll be the envy of your neighbours. And it'll only cost you £53 million.'

'HOW MUCH?' roared Daddy Bear. 'For an entirely superfluous door?'

'OK, absolutely the last thingymajig,' said Boris Johnson. 'I've told all the shops that surround this cottage that from now on you will no longer be buying anything from them.'

'Seriously?' shouted Baby Bear. 'Why did you do that?'

'Yeah,' agreed Mummy Bear. 'At least the other stuff had a sort of deranged whimsy to it. This just seems insane.'

'You don't need the rest of the town!' yelled Boris Johnson. 'This is a bold, exciting cottage with a long tradition of proud independence behind it. All this cottage needs is belief! Belief that it can deliver a prosperous future! A wonderful future! An I-feel-like-Chicken-Tonight future!'

'But we need to buy porridge,' said Mummy Bear.

'And a new chair to replace the one you broke with your arse,' said Baby Bear.

But Boris Johnson wasn't listening. He was too busy riffing on half-remembered old advertising slogans in lieu of saying anything substantive. So the bears did the only thing they could, and ate Boris Johnson.

The Optician of Barnard Castle

Once upon a time, there was a castle. And in that castle lived an optician; a kindly old man who wanted nothing more than to improve the sight of his townsfolk. Day after day he'd sit in his examination room, gesturing towards his charts and fastidiously switching lenses back and forth as he attempted to correct the various eye conditions he'd find himself presented with.

But then the sickness came, and the optician's custom began to dry up. The townsfolk were instructed to stay in their homes and prevent the spread of the disease, and appointments quickly dwindled. At a loss for things to do, the optician attempted new things to pass the time. He caught up on his reading list. He rearranged his examination room. He developed an interest in bonsai topiary. And yet nothing could replace his love for the ophthalmic sciences. He was lonely.

One night, two months into quarantine, the optician gazed out of his bedroom window and saw a shooting star blazing across the inky black sky. 'Shooting star, oh shooting star,' he said, 'How I wish I could treat patients again. Even just one.' Then he got into bed, pulled his duvet up to his ears and fell into a deep slumber.

The next morning he awoke to the sound of an almighty crash.

The optician sat bolt upright, fumbled for his glasses and ran downstairs in his pyjamas to discover the source of the commotion. And there he saw it, a crumpled and steaming Range Rover Discovery wrapped around a stone pillar beneath his window. The car was a write-off, and the optician feared the worst about the driver.

But then, miracles of miracles, the door opened and a man stepped out. He was like no sort of man the optician had ever seen before – his head looked like the grape you'd eat last from the bunch, and he was wearing clothing so bewilderingly mismatched that the optician assumed he had got dressed in a hurry at night to escape some sort of fire – but the important thing was that he was OK.

'Yeah, I'm pretty sure my eyes are buggered,' the

man shouted at the car as he looked around at his surroundings.

'Sir!' shouted the concerned optician. 'Sir, you appeared to have been in a terrible accident. Come inside, for I am medically trained.'

'Who said that?' yelled the man, looking around and squinting. 'Is that you, mother?'

'Your eyes are hurt, I understand,' said the optician as he placed a steadying hand on the man's shoulder. 'But this is a most fortuitous day indeed. You see, I am an optician, and in my examination room I have all the instruments that one needs to ...'

'Yeah, listen,' replied the man. 'I don't need an optician.'

The optician was flummoxed. 'B-but sir ...,' he stammered.

'That's what the drive was for, wasn't it?' snapped the man.

'Pardon?'

'The drive,' said the man, his patience starting to wear thin. 'I didn't know if my eyes were any good or not, so I went for a drive.'

'Yes,' replied the optician. 'You went for a drive to see an optician.'

'No,' said the man, 'Whenever I can't see properly, I like to hop in the car and aim at something big. What's an optician?'

The optician tried to hide his confusion. 'So you're local,' he asked.

There was a long pause. 'Sort of,' replied the man.

The man explained that he was very important, and very, very clever – the cleverest in all the land. In fact, he was an advisor to the king himself, although the optician didn't realise this at first, because the man kept referring to the king as 'that idiot'. He was due to drive back to London today, he said, but he wanted to check that his eyesight was OK, so he'd decided to embark on a sixty-minute road trip to be certain first.

'And you crashed,' said the optician.

'Yeah,' replied the man. He turned back towards the car. 'Told you my eyes were fucked, didn't I?' he shouted.

'Sir, you must have hurt your head in the crash,' said the optician. 'You are not addressing a person. That is a car, my friend.'

Then the passenger window rolled down. A woman poked her head out. 'What did you say?' she shouted at the man.

'My goodness!' cried the optician. 'You drove for sixty minutes with compromised eyesight with a passenger sitting next to you?'

'That's right,' said the man. 'That's my wife.'

The optician was staggered. 'Well, couldn't she have driven instead of you?' he cried at the man.

'Oh!' said the man. 'I hadn't thought of that.'

'DADDY!' shouted a voice from the back of the car, 'MY IPAD IS BROKEN!'

'Good God, there's a *child* in there too?' screamed the optician, unable to fathom what he was hearing.

'Of course there is. That's my son. He's four.'

'He's FOUR?!' yelled the optician. 'Is he strapped in safely at least?'

'I don't know,' replied the man. 'I can't see very well, can I?'

'I'M NOT!' shouted the boy.

'Listen, it's OK,' the man assured the optician. 'Technically my father owns the castle, so it's not like I'm breaking any rules.'

The optician was at a loss. In all his years he had never encountered such objectively arrogant stupidity.

'Well,' he eventually stammered. 'I suppose we should find out what's wrong with your eyes.'

'Oh, I know what's wrong with my eyes,' replied the man. 'It's the sickness.'

The optician yanked his hand from the man's shoulder as fast as he could. 'The SICKNESS?' he screamed.

'Oh yeah,' said the man. 'I'm really ill with it. We all are.' He rolled his eyes. 'That's why we're here in the first place.'

The optician began to sweat with fear. 'So, let me get this straight,' he said. 'You crashed your car this morning because you drove your family for an extended trip, in a town you're not from, while not only blind but infectious with the worst disease that humanity has faced in a century?'

'Yes,' shrugged the man.

'And you actually thought that any of this was OK?'

'What if I told you that I'm quite important?' offered the man.

'You're a monster!' the optician screamed. 'Of all the craven, thoughtless, self-interested morons I've ever had the displeasure of meeting, you are undoubtedly the worst. And now look at me. I'm just standing here breathing in all your germs. I am bound to get sick too. You have doomed me, sir. DOOMED ME!'

'Look, don't believe everything you hear at those press briefings,' said the man.

'WHAT?' cried the optician, before giving up. 'GOODBYE,' he shouted.

And the optician ran back to his examination room, slammed the door behind him, took off all his clothes, burned them, and then scrubbed at his hands with bleach until they began to bleed. He did not know if he would ever be well again.

Dominic Cummings stood next to his car, blinking in the sunshine and wondering how on earth he was going to spin this when the papers found out.

'Can I have my birthday cake now?' his wife asked through the window.

'Not now, Mary,' the man hissed.

The North Wind and the Sun, Part Two

'Best of three?'

It had been two thousand years since he had lost his bet with the Sun, and the North Wind was still smarting. Every single time he saw that stupid smug Sun, he was reminded of his own failure. Besides, the Sun was probably cheating anyway.

The rules of the bet, as he kept reminding the Sun, had been simple. They were to have a test of strength to see who could make a passing traveller lose his cloak the fastest. So the North Wind blew and blew, but every gust just made the traveller clutch his cloak more tightly to his body. And then the Sun – the poxy, no-good Sun – smiled a little, and his warmth made the traveller remove his cloak of his own accord. By the North Wind's reckoning, that isn't winning the bet; that's stiffing your pal on a loophole.

'Best of three?' he repeated.

'I really don't see the point, dear boy,' replied the Sun. 'This wasn't ever just a bet. It was a lesson, both to you and to the world in general. Brute strength only works up to a point. If you really want to make people do anything, you have to use kindness. I thought I'd made that perfectly clear.'

'Right, so what have you got to lose?' argued the North Wind. 'We'll try again, you'll win again and I'll have to lump it for another couple of millennia.'

'Oh fine,' replied the Sun. In truth he didn't really feel the need to prove anything to anyone, but it was winter, and he was bored, and at least he'd get to destroy someone's self-esteem for kicks.

The North Wind and the Sun huddled together to seek out a suitable candidate for their new test. Eventually, they found one. A ridiculous pinprick of a woman, a pathetic little mortal, carrying three bags of shopping down a quiet side street below. She was small, she was fallible and – most importantly – she wore a parka zipped all the way up to her chin.

'I really don't see the point of going through all this again,' sighed the Sun, 'but at least have the decency to let me go first this time. And don't get comfortable. This will only take a moment.'

And so the Sun gazed down at the woman below, with kindness and warmth in his eyes. As the temperature increased, the woman slowed to a standstill. She put her shopping bags down on the pavement next to her.

'There, you see?' chided the Sun. 'Piece of cake. Now let's never do this again.'

'Hold on a second,' said the North Wind. 'What's she doing?'

They both looked down at the woman. To the Sun's astonishment, she did not drop her bags to remove her coat. Instead, she reached into her pocket and pulled out her phone.

The Sun paused for a moment. Was something wrong? He'd done this before, after all, and it had worked like a dream. Undeterred, he smiled a little wider, and his rays grew a little warmer.

Still nothing. The North Wind and the Sun looked down at the woman and wondered what the problem was. Could it be, they pondered, that she had some sort of disfigurement that prevented her from removing her coat in public? Might she be a shoplifter, hiding her spoils underneath her outerwear? Maybe she just really liked coats? Who knew?

They watched as the woman opened a weather app on her phone.

'I've got you now,' said the Sun, and he grinned the

broadest grin he could. He grinned so hard that his cheeks began to hurt, and his teeth started to grind together, and a throbbing vein popped up on his forehead. The temperature grew hotter and hotter, but still the woman was too engrossed in her phone to unzip her coat.

'What's going on?' asked the North Wind.

'I don't know!' growled the Sun through gritted teeth, as his eyes began to water from the strain of all his gentle kindness.

Below, the woman was perplexed. 'It's the middle of winter,' she thought to herself. 'The weather was absolutely fine a minute ago, and now all of a sudden it's the hottest day of the year. This is berserk.'

The people around her all thought the same. One by one they slowed down and checked their weather apps as well. They began to glance over at each other with panic in their eyes, far too worried to even think about taking off their coats.

'Oh God, this is it, isn't it?' one of them sobbed.

'It must be!' wailed another. 'Go home and hug your children, everybody! The climate has finally reached extinction point! We're all doomed!'

It was pandemonium. The North Wind and the Sun looked down as cars began to crash into each other on the street and fist fights began to break out willy-nilly, as the entire population of Planet Earth ran and screamed and wept for their lives, convinced that the sixth great extinction was nigh.

'Oh, I've had enough of this,' said the North Wind. 'If you can't get rid of her coat, I will.'

And the North Wind blew. And the North Wind blew. Over and over again, he blew and blew and blew. He blew until the azure skies turned grey. He blew until his cheeks ached. But this did nothing to stop the panic raging below. If anything, it only exacerbated it.

'WHAT IS HAPPENING?' the people below yelled, whipped into a frenzy by all these sudden changes of extreme weather.

But the North Wind wouldn't give up. He blew harder than ever, until his gusts uprooted trees and flipped over cars. He looked down at the woman, but she had simply tucked into a doorway, shouting into her phone so as to be heard over the racket.

'Mum! Mum!' she cried. 'This is it! This is really it! This is the end of everything we've ever known. Oh, if only we had listened. Oh, if only we had heeded the warnings while we still had time. This is all our fault, Mum. Our greed, our stupidity, our horrible instinct to consume! This wasn't ever climate change, Mum! This was suicide!'

The North Wind and the Sun looked at each other, flummoxed.

'Call it a draw?' asked the Sun.

'Yeah, screw this,' replied the North Wind. 'Pint?'

'Yeah,' sighed the Sun. 'You're buying.'

And with that, all the awful weather on Earth slowed and stopped. The wind receded. The heat cooled. Within minutes it was a normal winter's day again. The woman looked up at the sky in wonderment.

'Hang on a minute,' she shouted at the Sun and the Wind. 'Are you telling me that all this extreme weather, all these droughts and floods and tornadoes, the melting ice caps and species driven to extinction were just down to you pair of morons being a bit alpha with each other? Really? This was never our fault?'

She grabbed a passing stranger by the shoulders. 'Do you hear? This was never our fault! We were all feeling guilty for nothing. We didn't have to stop using plastic straws after all. I ate all that tofurkey for nothing! If only we'd known that nothing we do ever has any sort of negative consequence whatsoever! We're free! Free!'

And with that the woman made a great big pile of tyres and disposable nappies and car batteries, and she set them all on fire. And as the fire sent billowing wafts of toxic smoke into the atmosphere, she danced for joy.

And they all lived happily ever after, especially Greta Thunberg because all this meant she could finally just get on with being a teenager again.

What Do People in your Bubble Do All Day?

Once upon a time, there was a general election. An opinion poll said the result was going to be close, maybe even creating a hung parliament.

But Joshua the florist wanted to be certain, so he asked all his friends how they intended to vote. This is what they said.

Henry the lawyer said he was voting for the nice party.

Nigel the university lecturer said he was voting for the nice party.

Ophelia the doctor said she was voting for the nice party.

Jemima the online documentary-maker said she was voting for the nice party.

Ryan the wealthy television actor said he was voting for the nice party.

Oliver the left-wing newspaper columnist said he was voting for the nice party.

Harold, who made non-profit apps for the disadvantaged, said he was voting for the nice party.

Kate, who worked in publishing, said she was voting for the nice party.

Sebastian the small-batch baker said he was voting for the nice party.

Felicity the mumtrepreneur said she was voting for the nice party.

Pia the Airbnb superhost said she was voting for the nice party.

Verity, who had an Etsy page selling gingham fairies in various poses, said she was voting for the nice party.

Lizzy the woke podcaster said she was voting for the nice party.

Will the independent bookseller said he was voting for the nice party.

Daniel the panel-show comedian said he was voting for the nice party.

Richard, who had a charity that organised horse-stroking sessions for the medically anxious, said he was voting for the nice party.

Lance the upcycler said he was voting for the nice party.

Fabian the Deliveroo driver said he was voting for the nice party.

Johan the liveblogger said he was voting for the nice party.

Valentina, who owned a decorative belt-buckle subscription delivery firm, said she was voting for the nice party.

Kevin, who sold pots of handmade honey at the local farmer's market, said he was voting for the nice party.

Bryony, who soothed distressed moles for a living, said she was voting for the nice party.

Zane the Instagram influencer said he was voting for the nice party.

Maxwell the beard-oil impresario said he was voting for the nice party.

Fabio the satirical wedding DJ said he was voting for the nice party.

Barney, who sold expensive offal products in a pop-up restaurant inside a condemned glue factory, said he was voting for the nice party.

Camille, who recycled used tampons into school equipment for Africa, said she was voting for the nice party.

Jason, who was the vice chairman of his father's graphic design company, said he was voting for the nice party.

Belinda, who owned an antique brass trombone showroom, said she was voting for the nice party.

Rachel, who worked at a biscuit start-up, said she was voting for the nice party.

Jessica the online content facilitator said she was voting for the nice party.

Derek the ironic hairdresser said he was voting for the nice party.

Penelope, who performed topical burlesque routines to disinterested patrons in an abandoned working men's club, said she was voting for the nice party.

All Joshua's friends, in fact, said they were voting for the nice party.

And then election day came. And the nice party won by a landslide. And everybody lived happily ever after. This is a fairy tale, after all.

The Snowflake

Once upon a time there was a snowflake. An actual snowflake, who lived in a cloud.

For some reason, everyone hated the snowflake. One day, a prominent middle-aged newspaper columnist wrote a column about his dislike of the snowflake, entitled 'Why the snowflake represents everything bad about the modern age'.

This caused people to intensify their own feelings about the snowflake. Facebook began to fill with people angrily comparing their own struggles to the comparatively mild struggles of the snowflake.

'In my day we played outside,' they wrote. 'Our parents didn't know where we were, nor did they care. We didn't play with iPads because we were all outside hitting each other with sticks. Can the snowflake honestly say this about its childhood?'

But the snowflake could not, because it was a snowflake.

Attacks started pouring in from all directions. On breakfast television one morning, an outspoken host was presenting a segment about meat. 'I love steak!' he crowed, chewing noisily. 'I bet you don't love steak, do you snowflake? I bet meat just offends you.'

But the snowflake didn't have any opinion about meat because it had never tasted meat. It was a snowflake. It wouldn't have a clue what to do if you stuck a steak in front of it because it didn't have a digestive system. It was a snowflake.

'Look at me!' cried a sixty-three-year-old man who had deliberately dressed himself in a weirdly non-specific amalgamation of Asian and African garments to prove some sort of nebulous point about freedom of speech. 'I bet you can't stand this! I bet you think it's cultural appropriation, don't you snowflake?'

But the snowflake didn't respond, because it didn't understand the concept of cultural appropriation, on the basis that it was just a flake of snow in the sky.

'Don't clap too loudly!' sneered an edgy comedian as he walked onstage to an audience of guffawing dads. 'This is supposed to be a "safe space". We wouldn't want to trigger the poor snowflake now, would we?'

But the snowflake was not triggered because it was a snowflake. It was literally just an actual snowflake. I honestly don't see what's so hard to understand about this. It was a snowflake.

'You'll never buy a house if you spend all your money on avocado toast!' people shouted at the snowflake.

'I'm sick of all your pious virtue signalling!' people shouted at the snowflake.

'God help us if there's a war!' people shouted at the snowflake.

Soon the whole world was full of angry people screaming hatred into the sky, based on nothing but an incorrect assumption that the snowflake was somehow either sentient or responsible for society-wide progress that had caused them to become fearful of their place in the world. On and on they shouted, for days and days and days.

As the snowflake drifted downwards, it saw that it would land in a plastic cup occupied by a several other snowflakes, swimming in a thick gloopy liquid. As it floated closer, it was able to make out the words on the side of the cup: Salted Caramel Banana Milkshake. 'Finally,' thought the milkshake: 'I'm home.'

Planet Kondo

Once upon a time, there was a woman named Marie Kondo. Marie was a millennial icon, thanks to her radical ideas about minimalistic living. According to Marie, if a possession of yours failed to 'spark joy' when you touched it, you must instantly throw it out. If you did this then, little by little, you would gradually rid your house of clutter and eventually live calmly and cleanly, surrounded by only your most treasured items.

It was a wonderful idea with only one drawback: thanks to Marie Kondo, everyone in the world threw out ninety per cent of their possessions at exactly the same time.

Suddenly the streets became overrun with old cardigans and Tupperware lids. Scores of Ethernet cables and USB-powered cup heaters clogged up all the tips and landfills.

Mile-high tidal waves of old Christmas cards and digital cameras and not-quite-nostalgic-enough-to-keep Beanie Babies rampaged through the countryside.

The seas became choked on a tangle of reed diffusers and unused curtain rings and denim jackets and plastic cutlery and 2016 calendars and Post-It Notes and Happy Meal toys and iPhone headphone jack connectors and Instant Pots and NutriBullets and odd socks and Dunelm catalogues and novelty vases and Duplo.

Our homes were empty, but the environment was a mess. Put simply, planet Earth was overwhelmed.

The problem was so acute that various NGOs came up with all manner of potential solutions. The major fashion houses declared that the next big trend would be ethically recycled clothes, and set about making a series of coats and blouses and trousers all knitted together from scraps of dishcloths and bunting and unloved puppets. This approach initially worked, but it backfired when people took them home, touched them, realised that they didn't spark joy and threw them straight back out again.

One charity attempted to repurpose some of the discarded possessions to help the homeless, but all the homeless people pointed out in the strongest possible terms that the last things they needed were an inflatable chair and a bucket of lower-tier Beanie Babies.

At one point Kevin Costner declared that he'd invented a rubbish-eating machine, but that turned out to be nonsense. Planet Earth was doomed.

In the end, NASA had an idea. They called a huge press conference and announced that the only way to save the planet was to collect every last discarded item in a giant net and drag it into space behind an enormous rocket. Once it had reached a safe distance from our solar system, it would be unleashed and enter the universe as a new heavenly body. Again, they announced, there was only one drawback: the rocket needed a pilot, and the pilot would never make their way back to Earth. It was, in effect, a suicide mission.

'麻里恵さんはこの宇宙船を操縦したいのです,' piped up a small voice from the back of the room.

Everyone turned around to see none other than Marie Kondo herself, who had snuck in by wearing a beard made of knitted toilet-roll cosies. 'Marie wishes to pilot this craft,' repeated her translator in English.

The room fell silent. The head of NASA explained once more that this was a death sentence. If she flew the giant rubbish bag into space, she'd perish, cold and alone in the distant blackness of the universe.

'片づけるのは麻里恵さんに決まっています', replied Marie Kondo. '彼女は散らかっているものが大嫌いなんですよ.'

'Marie wishes it to be known that this is her mess,' said the translator. 'And she really hates mess.'

It was decided.

And so, three months later, Marie Kondo sat atop a custom-built rocket tied to a ball of trash as big as a mountain. The responsibility was huge. She only had one shot to get this right.

Silence fell around her. 'Ready for ignition?' asked a disembodied voice in her helmet.

'どうかときめいてくださいよ,' replied Marie Kondo.

Inside Mission Control, the head of NASA turned to Marie's translator. 'What did she say?' he asked.

'She ... she asked you to spark joy,' replied the translator with tears streaming down her face.

'Consider our joy sparked,' whispered the head of NASA, and he pressed the button.

Up through the clouds hurtled Kondo and her giant sphere of crap. Through the clouds she soared into the inky twilight of space.

Slowly the hours turned into days, and the days into weeks, as Kondo blasted across the galaxy. As the weeks turned into months, she found herself asking profound questions of her life's work. *Is a clean home worth the destruction of everything around it?* she wondered. *Would the world have been better off if people remained slightly untidy?* Kondo looked out at the cleanly beautiful desolation of deep space, and she saw herself staring back.

After six years in space, the engines on Kondo's rockets finally sputtered out. Kondo swept back her incredibly long hair – scissors having been one thing she neglected to take with her, on account of their inability to spark joy. She took one last look around the interior of her ship and smiled at the neat way that all her faecal containers had been stacked up against the rear wall. She put on her space suit one last time, opened the airlock and stepped out into the infinite void. It was time, at last, to release the net.

With her final gasps of oxygen, Kondo disengaged the rubbish from the rocket. She looked back. Earth was light years behind her, but she took small consolation from the knowledge that, by sacrificing her life, she had ultimately become its saviour.

As her vision faded, Marie Kondo felt a sensation of being held tightly. The cold darkness of space was replaced by a warm white light. She was filled with a sense of total peace; a peace she had been working towards her whole life.

'ここは、もしかして天国ですか,' she wondered. 'Is this heaven?'

Then an alien lurched into her field of vision. 'Lady, is that a Teddy Ruxpin?' it asked.

Marie Kondo blinked. As she looked around, she

came to understand what had happened. An alien spacecraft had stopped alongside her at her moment of death, pulled her on board and revived her. She squinted at the alien.

'This thing here,' the alien repeated. 'Is it an M&S Royal Jubilee reusable tote bag?'

'And that?' asked a second alien, peering out of the spaceship's window. 'Is that an iSight webcam? I've been looking for one of those since Apple withdrew FireWire support in 2008. How much do you want for it?'

'Yeah, and I'll take that bundle of empty Quality Street tubs as well please,' added the first alien.

At this point, Marie Kondo realised that she had invented the universe's first intergalactic boot fair. Nothing, not a single piece of the tat that she'd flown into deep space, went unsold. Smiling, Kondo realised that everything, no matter how pointless, can spark joy in someone. And they all lived happily ever after.

Gulliver's Travels in Thanet

My father was part of the metropolitan elite, as was his father before him. As such, my life was full of the struggles that most everyday people face: buying copies of the Saturday *Guardian* that didn't contain the Yotam Ottolenghi sumac supplement as advertised; having to buy a £15 rye loaf from Ally Pally Farmer's Market because all the £18 sourdough loaves were sold out; getting a dry throat from telling everyone that I don't own a television.

But unlike my father and his father before him, I yearned to see the wider world. Growing up, I was told all manner of tall tales about exotic lands that existed beyond the comfortable boundaries of Crouch End: far-flung destinations like Watford and Croydon and Penge. I was told that these were dangerous and wild territories, full of thugs and villains and something called a Poundstretcher. To leave the confines of N8 would be to encounter a morass of savage ugliness, I was told, and I took these warnings to heart.

Then fate intervened. One spring, I accepted an advantageous offer from my friend Dan – a free-lance shoe designer – to accompany him on an ironic Groupon sightseeing tour upon the River Thames, during which we would partake in the traditional ironic Groupon activities: discussing negronis, tweeting half-thought one-liners about the news and quietly mocking anyone who sincerely appeared to be having fun.

It would not be proper to trouble the reader with the particulars of our adventures; let it suffice to inform them that in our passage we were driven by a violent storm all the way out towards Dartford. The wind was so strong that the boat fell apart among the frothing waters, and my last recollection of this terrible ordeal was when I, with my last breath of strength, clambered atop some driftwood and soon passed out.

I awoke, ravaged and shaken, washed up on a beach; a sandy crescent stretch that bore the pungent stench of sugar and vegetable oil. My head was pounding, but when I tried to raise my hand in an expression of simple self-care, I found that I could not. My arms and legs were fastened on each side to the ground, and I likewise felt several ligatures across my body, from my armpits to my thighs.

In my position I could see nothing but the drizzled sky, and hear nothing but the distant strains of what sounded like a seventeen-year-old *Time Crisis 3* arcade console stuck in a perpetual loop of its demonstration mode. As I tugged at the ropes lashing me to the sand, a commotion stirred around me.

Cries of *Oozat!* and *Wossawlvis?* cracked out through the slate-grey sky, as I felt the dull thud of a size eight Nike Air VaporMax Plus crash into my ribs. 'Sirs!' I cried, 'I beseech you! I am but a weary traveller in this monstrous domain! Would you perhaps supply me with a flat white with which to revive my senses?' This request, however, was met with naught but more grunting and intolerable strikes against my person.

After a concerted effort on my part to turn my neck just two inches, I was greeted by the most incredible sight. A crowd of twenty or thirty creatures; almost human-looking, yet clad from head to toe in what can only be described as nylon sportswear. They had about them the confused demeanour of apes, and yet one was gripped by the presence of an underlying intelligence. Oh, the things these curious beings could tell us, I thought, if only they had the ability to communicate.

I realised immediately that my requests for a flat white were too sophisticated for these lumpen oafs. With as much decency as I could muster, I struck upon a plan of non-verbal communication. Looking each of the creatures in the eye, I slowly and deliberately licked my lips to better demonstrate my thirst.

It took a few moments to register my desire – at first my gestures were met with confused grunts of *Puhvurt!* and *Wankor!* – until the figure I took to be the leader corrected his underlings. *Nahmate*, he said with a compassionate nod, *Monsa! Monsa!*

There was a flurry of activity around me as the ropes tying me down were loosened. I was handed a metal cylinder – much like the cans of imported IPA I had enjoyed with Dan at the start of my fateful voyage – that bore the inscription 'MONSTER ENERGY'. Parched, and with no other option available, I opened my mouth and consumed this foul concoction, which tasted like someone had diluted dishwater with a bucket of rancid Calpol. But I knew better than to show any outward signs of disgust; instead I nodded and made an overblown 'mmm' sound.

This seemed to work. The creatures untied me completely and helped me to my feet. I took out my iPhone, intending to check Google Maps to discern my whereabouts, but this triggered a wave of enthusiasm among the natives. They began whooping and hopping from foot to foot with excitement, showing me their phones in what I believed to be an attempt to reach common ground. Their naivety was touching

– their phones were older, squatter models, some dating as far back as 2015 – but I took it as a sign of affection nonetheless. I held the phone to my ear. 'Hello? Hello?' I pantomimed, and they did the same. *Ullo! Ullo!* they called back, idiotic grins plastered across their awful faces. Finally, a connection!

I could live here, I thought. I could educate these savages. Chances are they'd never tasted quinoa, or ridden a Brompton, or compiled a Spotify playlist of politicised funk music from the 1970s. I could be their leader, I realised. I could be the great enlightener, just like the explorers of ...

'Jeremy, look!'

My reverie was cut short by the sight of a young family – a real, recognisable human family, with complicated shoes and an unnecessarily bulky buggy of Swedish manufacture – running towards me. Their sudden appearance spooked the creatures, who promptly ran off. I was sad to see them go, these pathetic wastrels. Our time together was brief, but I consoled myself with the knowledge that we had experienced a moment of true connection.

But nevertheless I was overjoyed to see these people, these actual people, who grabbed me and patted me and soothed me with coffee. They took me to an adequate sourdough pizza restaurant, sat me down and explained that I had arrived in a land called Margate.

As I had assumed, they told me that it was a gruesome land full of catalogue shops and UKIP voters, but my new friends reassured me that they were already in the process of colonising it. Their intention was to drive up the house prices and force the natives to live in a nearby hovel known as Gillingham. They would be happier there, they explained, and I thanked them for all their good work.

As my countrymen escorted me to the train station to begin my long journey home, I asked them for a selfie so as to never forget my incredible adventure. They obliged, and my eyes pricked with grateful tears.

My father and my father's father were wrong. There is a whole world outside of London, I had discovered, but it wasn't scary at all. The creatures I'd met were tribal and frightened, but much more like me than I had ever expected. Maybe deep down, I thought, we really *are* all just the same as each other. We are all trying to make do with whatever miserable hand fate has dealt us. I vowed to return to Margate at the earliest convenience, to further blur the lines that once divided us.

As my train pulled away from the station, I became aware of a commotion on the platform. Well, if it wasn't the creatures from the beach! As I turned to face them, I saw them leaping and running, holding up a tattered copy of the *New Statesman* that must have fallen out of my jacket pocket at some point. *Fankoo! Fankoo!* they hooted with innocent glee, as they clumsily slapped at a quick-turnaround think piece about transphobia.

'No, strange creatures of Margate,' I thought to myself as the train sped onwards, 'you have opened my eyes. Fank *ooo.*' And with that, I opened up the Rightmove app on my phone.

The Very Trendy Caterpillar

In the light of the moon, a little egg lay on a leaf.

One Sunday morning, the warm sun came up and POP! – out of the egg came a tiny and very hungry hipster.

He started to look for some food.

On Monday he ate through one vegan sausage roll, but he was still hungry.

On Tuesday he ate through two charcoal ice creams, but he was still hungry.

On Wednesday he ate through three cannabidiol protein bars, but he was still hungry.

On Thursday he slurped through four turmeric lattes served in avocado shells, but he was still hungry.

On Friday he ate through five bowls of imported breakfast cereal, paid for by the gram as if it was some kind of exotic street drug, but he was still hungry.

On Saturday he ate through one plate of squoodles, one *imagawayaki*, one handful of legumes prescribed to him by a nutritionist who believed that people should eat according to blood type, one bakeable custard-flavour Japanese Kit-Kat, one Funfetti birthday cake, one piece of ketogenic cauliflower pizza, one salted caramel freakshake, one jug of sipping vinegar, one serving of Guatemalan kak'ik manufactured by two privately educated Englishmen who spent some of their gap year living three countries away from Guatemala, and one slice of jackfruit. That night he had a stomach ache!

The next day was Sunday again. The caterpillar gave himself a salt-water flush, and after that he felt much better.

Now he was no longer hungry, nor a little hipster. He was a big, fat hipster.

He built a small house around himself, called a cocoon, and he stayed inside for more than two weeks.

Then he nibbled a hole in the cocoon, pushed his way out, and he was a beautiful butterfly. However, during his time spent inside the cocoon, the internet had burned through so many dumb new food fads that the butterfly felt old and irrelevant and just started eating chips again. Finally, he was happy.

The Little Tweet That Could

Once upon a time, there lived an evil king.

The king was cruel; vain and greedy and obsessed with gold. His ways were unlike those of any of the kings who had come before him. Although his subjects had provided him with a glittering white palace, he preferred to live on a golf course in Florida.

Strangest of all was his crown, a tattered thing that sat atop his head, seemingly made of pubic hair. If one of his subjects so much as looked at his crown, the king would fly into a violent rage and imprison them in his castle's dungeon. Lots of people looked at his crown, so his dungeon was always full.

Everything the king did was cruel. He hated anyone who did not live in his kingdom, and built a huge wall to keep out all the foreigners. He made his subjects pay vast sums of gold for medicine that the rest of the world got for free. He surrounded himself with his cruel family; Princess Ivanka, Prince King Jr, and his mutant son Eric, who he kept chained to his throne at all times. His wife, Queen Melania, had only smiled once in her entire life, and that was on the day that the king started choking on a fish bone and it briefly looked as if he might die. They were a terrible, evil, no-good family.

Worst of all, nobody could stop them. Many people tried. Constable Mueller from the local police force tried to arrest the king, but it didn't work. Mayor Pelosi from City Hall did such sarcastic clapping at one of his speeches that it became a viral meme. The local scholars released scroll after scroll informing the population that the king didn't pay his taxes, but nobody read them. Just before his coronation, several millionaire actors made a YouTube video of them singing a song with obliquely defiant lyrics, but not even this could prevent the king's terrible rampage of destruction.

The king was a lonely, reclusive man. When he wanted to address his subjects, he didn't do it face-to-face like all the previous kings had. No, he did it with tweets.

The tweets were relentless. 'My enemies are pigs and loozers,' they read. 'Scrolls are FAKE NEWS and a total disgrace,' they read. 'Everyone who is not from this kingdom is a criminal and a rapist – especially the children. ONLY YOUR KING CAN SAVE YOU,' they read. Day after day after day, the kingdom trembled in fear under this non-stop bombardment.

But one day a young charity worker named Stephanie, who lived in the small village of Williamsburg, Brooklyn, read the king's tweets on her MacBook. The tweets made her very sad.

'Catch my enemies and detain their children before our kingdom is put in great danger,' she read aloud in horror. 'KINGDOM FIRST!'

Stephanie put down her coffee and looked across the table at her boyfriend, a thirty-two-year-old man who described himself on LinkedIn as a DJ even though he worked full-time as a lettings agent. 'This king is cruel,' she said. 'I must remind him of this immediately.'

'But why?' replied her boyfriend. 'Everyone has already tried to stop the king, but he's just too powerful. Plus, no one will read your tweet. You only have 150 followers, Stephanie'.

'No,' said Stephanie. 'Enough is enough. The time for talking is over. The king's terrible reign must come to an end now. If I have to be the one to change things, then so be it.'

Stephanie's boyfriend smirked. 'Sure,' he told her, sarcastically. 'You do what you think is best.' Then he went back to toying with the wireless Beats headphones that he always wore around his neck despite rarely actually using them. Stephanie was used to this sort of reaction. She'd been undermined her whole life. But not today.

Stephanie quietly collected up all her ill feeling towards the king, all the fear and hurt that he'd caused during his malevolent reign, and pushed it out through the tips of her fingers. With an overwhelming sense of duty, she tapped out a reply:

'Detaining 👋 children 👋 is 👋 bad 👋 imo.'

★ ★ ★

As soon as Stephanie pressed send, the brave little tweet was fired straight into the internet. Instantly, it was terrified. Is this what the internet was? Wherever it looked, it was overcome with horrors: Nazis and dick pics and bomb-making tutorials and people arguing about stuff that Piers Morgan had said specifically to get a reaction.

The tweet's first instinct was to quit; to run back into Stephanie's computer and quiver behind an error message. 'But no,' it thought. 'I am an important message. I have to do my job.'

Soon enough, the tweet found its way towards the king's mentions. But even that was overwhelming, since the king's mentions were full of fury and racism and Russian bots. What were the chances of Stephanie's tweet even being seen? Minimal at best. 'But no,' thought the tweet. 'I have to do my job. I have to.'

★ ★ ★

Back at the castle the king's phone pinged. Curious, he drew it up close to his squinty little eyes and saw an alert. It read: 'New reply from @quinoafan1988: "Detaining children is bad imo."'

With more agility than he had ever demonstrated, the king ran straight into his daughter's bedroom.

'Princess Ivanka!' the king cried, handing her the phone. 'Read this message! Someone just dared tell me that I shouldn't detain immigrant children! It's an outrage!'

The princess read the message. 'I mean, it kind of is cartoonishly evil,' she replied with a thin smile.

The king was displeased. He grabbed the phone and ran into his wife's bedroom. 'Queen Melania!' he yelled. 'You won't believe this, but somebody has questioned my authority on the internet.'

'WHY YOU STILL ALIVE OLD MAN?' Queen Melania shouted.

The king's head was swimming. What was happening? Why was everybody suddenly turning against him? He ran into Eric's bedroom. 'Eric, I ...'

'Bloooorfffff,' replied Eric.

'Never mind,' said the king. Eric had always been a disappointment.

Stunned, the king staggered back into his throne room. Is this really what the world thought about him, he wondered. Was he really as evil as everyone said?

He sat and thought about his actions; about everything he'd done to keep his kingdom safe. Sure, perhaps there were times when he may have been a little heavy-handed, but surely everyone could see that he was just acting in the kingdom's interest.

Then he thought about the children he'd detained. He thought about their mothers and fathers, scared and frantic, and for the first time put himself in their shoes. How would he feel if his children were taken from him? He thought about life without Ivanka or Prince King Jr, and his heart felt true sadness. This was a new feeling, and it crushed him. How could he ever have been so cruel? He was a monster.

Then he thought about life without Eric and just sort of shrugged but, hey, a first step is a first step.

Shaken to his very core, the king walked out to the balcony of his castle and – for the first time – addressed his subjects face-to-face.

'I have been a fool,' he shouted to the crowds below. 'A sad, mean, old fool. Thanks to this tweet I just got sent, I can see now that I have caused you great suffering. I have caused everyone great suffering. And now, my kingdom, I must atone. Starting immediately, I order all the detained children to be reunited with their parents!'

The crowds cheered.

'Furthermore, all medicine from this point onwards will be free at the point of delivery!' he roared.

The crowds cheered harder.

'And, what the hell, let's ban all the blunderbusses too!'

The crowds cheered and danced and sang. This was a great day. A wonderful day! The king had finally seen the error of his ways. For the rest of his reign, the king was happy and generous and beloved by all his subjects. Change really was possible after all.

* * *

Stephanie's tweet brought her great acclaim. Millions of people around the world credited her with changing the course of the kingdom itself, and she spent the rest of her life writing bestselling books about the power of the underdog. Soon she was the richest woman in the kingdom. She could afford everything she ever wanted. Except her own apartment, obviously. Let's not get too ridiculous.

Where Should We Live Now?

Mr and Mrs Smith wanted to move house. The rise of populist nationalist sentiment in Britain made them sad, so they sold their house and moved to France.

But the rise of Marine Le Pen's far-right National Rally party made them sad, so they moved to Italy.

But the anti-Europe coalition between the Five Star Movement and Lega Nord made them sad, so they moved to Denmark.

But the Danish government's policy of allowing its police to seize migrants' property to pay for their upkeep made them sad, so they moved to Hungary.

But Viktor Orbán's warnings about Europe losing its identity due to immigration made them sad, so they moved to Poland.

But the Law and Justice Party's policy of sacking

judges made them sad, so they moved to Sweden.

But the rise of the Swedish Democrat Party, which has its roots in neo-Nazism, made them sad, so they moved to Belarus.

But Alexander Lukashenko's suppression of his opponents, along with his statement that appeared to praise Hitler, made them sad, so they moved to Austria.

But the Freedom Party's proposals to ban head-scarves for schoolgirls and seize migrants' phones made them sad, so they moved to Germany.

But the Alternative for Germany party's habit of shrugging off Nazi atrocities as 'bird poo' made them sad, so they moved to Macedonia.

But the VMRO-DPMNE's policy of creating a tier system of race based on a vague notion of antiquisation made them sad, so they moved to Bulgaria.

But the fact that there is literally a far-right Bulgarian party called Attack made them sad, so they moved to the Czech Republic.

But they didn't like the rumours that Andrej Babiš kidnapped his own son in order to stop him giving evidence in a fraud enquiry, so they moved to Greece.

But Golden Dawn's swastika-aping logo and habit of denouncing homosexuality as a sickness made them sad, so they moved to the Philippines.

But all of Rodrigo Duterte's self-confessed

extrajudicial murders made them sad, so they moved to Brazil.

But Jair Bolsonaro's homophobia, misogyny and support for political violence made them sad, so they moved to America.

But as you can imagine that didn't really work out either.

It didn't matter where Mr and Mrs Smith went, because every single country in the world had a horrible streak of populist nationalism running right the way through it. Everywhere was just as bad as everywhere else.

So Mr and Mrs Smith bought a floating cargo ship, and they filled it with all the friends they had made on their travels, and together they all became the nicest, most tolerant, most progressive pirates on the seven seas. The ship became the most perfect democracy in the world, and everyone was happy, and if this boat actually exists can someone let me know because Jesus Christ.

Kanako the Instagram Hedgehog vs The United Nations

Instagram had given Kanako the hedgehog a good life. As one of the world's most beloved online animals, all Kanako had to do each day was to pose for photographs. Sometimes she'd nestle into a teacup, other times she'd sit atop a sumptuous pile of cashmere. She'd even started to fall asleep during photo shoots, and if anything this only made her more popular. 'Magic sleepy hedgehog of my heart!' the comments underneath her photos would read. 'Marry me Kanako!'

Of course, those days were gone now. Ever since the United Nations banned Instagram in a bid to reduce squandered global productivity, Kanako was useless. Without Instagram, her cuteness counted for nothing.

It didn't matter that her eyes glittered like snow on a silent winter's morning. It didn't matter that her spines were submerged in buffalo milk on a twice-monthly basis. It didn't matter that she'd learned how to make a noise that sounded like the word 'cuddle' specifically to drive up social media engagement. She was on the scrapheap, and she knew it.

Luckily, she'd fallen in with a few like-minded friends. Agnes the kitten, Mr Boompy the chipmunk and Pia the hat-wearing pig were also rendered redundant by the Instagram ban, and together they lived in a hollowed-out tree trunk on the edge of the park. It was adorable, and the fact that nobody even bothered to take photos of that sort of thing any more was legitimately heartbreaking.

Still, at least they could eat. Whenever the friends got peckish, they could simply help themselves to the vast piles of discarded avocados that now lined the streets. Without Instagram, everyone had stopped pretending that avocados tasted nice, and they just sat around eating Double Deckers in their pants instead.

But avocados were just the tip of the iceberg. The barista industry had cratered, the admission bar having been set low enough to include anyone who could pour some stuff into a cup, rather than pour some stuff into a cup and then draw a sort of leaf thing on top of it. Restaurants had abandoned the notion of presentation altogether, so the top dish served at famed Basque restaurant Asador Etxebarri now consisted of half a pint of runny mash hosed into a plastic bucket. The entire Kardashian family, wounded by their sudden lack of validation, were forced to crawl around Calabasas on their hands and knees begging strangers to put little red heart stickers on their faces and bodies.

Worst of all, though, was the birth rate. After all, what was the point of having children if you couldn't publish photos of them on the internet? Keep them clean? Listen to their ideas? Yuck.

But the United Nations couldn't be shifted. It pointed to the statistics: since banning Instagram, people had regained the ability to work without distraction. They rediscovered how to follow the plot lines of challenging prestige television series. Couples had started talking to each other again. Road deaths caused by people just wandering out into the street had fallen to almost zero.

This infuriated Kanako. Her entire raison d'être was Instagram. Without Instagram there was nothing to separate her from all the other hedgehogs, even the really crap ones who slept under bonfires. She was determined to change things.

'But what can we do?' asked Mr Boompy, absent-mindedly pushing a polystyrene snowman around in a miniature shopping trolley out of habit. 'This is the

United Nations we're talking about. They're a huge organisation, and we're just four stupid animals.'

'Hold on a second,' said Pia. 'Agnes, weren't you a goodwill ambassador for the UN a couple of years ago?'

'Well, I wouldn't call it that,' replied Agnes, who had simply taken part in an influencer campaign that literally consisted of her wearing a T-shirt with 'Landmines are bad' written on it. Nevertheless, she made a call and succeeded in securing Kanako a session at the UN headquarters.

But Kanako was worried. She'd heard of Secretary-General António Guterres before, and had been told many stories of his cold disinterest in cute internet animals. Even if she did get her day in the spotlight – and even if she did dress up in her most formal miniature top hat and wedding dress for it – it was obvious that Guterres would laugh Kanako out of the room.

And so Kanako did something that she'd never once thought to do before: she went to the library. And there she spent day after day poring over heavy-duty legal texts, to better present her case to the world. She read Directive (EU) 2018/1972 of the European Parliament, which worked to establish the European Electronic Communication Code. She read the Association of Progressive Communications' Global Information Society Watch, along with transcripts of workshops held at the 2018 Internet Governance Forum. She even watched several addresses from the UN's very own Internet Governance Forum, such was her determination to right this terrible wrong.

Meanwhile, her fellow tree-trunk chums went about rounding up as many other abandoned Instagram animals as they could, hoping that a united front could sway the mind of Guterres. They travelled around the world recruiting creature after creature, like Jaxxon the sloth, Simples the meerkat, Edwin the Rescue Goat, Nugget the beluga whale, Sparklebuck the mandarin duck, Jumbozara the Patagonian mara, Plonk-Plonk the giant panda, Snoochie the fennec fox, Admiral Snuggles von Chunkybum the pygmy hippopotamus, and Stephen the otter.

Together all the animals reached out to other noted Instagram stars – the coffee merchants, the avocado trade, the performative dads, the people who only go to protests because they've thought of an adequate pun that they can write on a placard, the people who wrongly assume that they are the first in the entire world to have ever seen a sunset, Ariana Grande – and they formed a union, because they understood the power of collective bargaining in the face of anonymous authority.

And then the day came for Kanako to give her speech to the UN General Assembly. All her allies sat in the back as she made her way up the staircase to her bespoke podium. An expectant hush fell across the room. Kanako adjusted her top hat.

'Ladies and gentlemen,' she began, 'while it is an honour to be invited to speak in such auspicious environs, I am afraid that the current situation simply must not stand.'

Over a barnstorming half-hour session, Kanako argued that the Instagram ban went against the egalitarian principles upon which the entire internet was founded, adding that – though initiated with the best intentions – it had negatively impacted on the livelihoods of millions.

'I mean, look at her,' Kanako said, gesturing towards one of the lower-division Kardashian sisters, who was tearfully using one her shoes to try to take a selfie. 'This is what your ban has done to people. It's inhumane.'

Then Kanako dropped her biggest bombshell of all; invoking the UN's own 'Report of the Special Rapporteur on the promotion and protection of the right to freedom of opinion and expression from 2011'. 'Was it not Section IV, part A, paragraph 31 that described online censorship as "an unnecessary or disproportionate means to achieve the purported aim" that is "frequently in violation of [its] obligation to guarantee the right to freedom of expression"?' Kanako squeaked adorably. 'Ladies and gentlemen, I put it to you that it was.'

A stunned silence fell across the floor. Kanako knew

that she had everyone right in the palm of her paw. One last strike and this would all be over. She yawned, stretched and made a noise that sounded a bit like the word 'cuddle'.

The room burst into waves of spontaneous applause. Secretary-General António Guterres, with tears in his eyes, walked onstage and hugged Kanako. Then he said 'ouch' and pressed a big red button to unban Instagram.

Immediately, people started eating avocado and drinking elaborate coffee and having babies again. All the animals went straight back to work, safe in the knowledge that the formal organisation of their industry would protect them for years to come.

And as for Kanako? She left modelling behind and went to college to further her studies. She's still on the internet if you want to find her, only now she's known as Kanako the Instagram Hedgehog: Doctor of Law.

Your Parents' Favourite Lullaby

Beautiful baby, it's time for some sleep
I know we've had fun, but it's late
Your eyelids are heavy, you're all tuckered out
And also you're now twenty-eight

You're so very precious, you light up our lives
This we thought you should know
But now you've grown up and you should have left
   home
Roughly a decade ago

This room where you sleep, it's technically ours
We've told you again and again
We love you completely, you're part of our hearts
But Dad's got his eye on a den

Your hair is like gold, kid, your eyes are like jewels
Your skin is just so luminescent
You're here on our dime, though, we feed you for
    free
You're getting to be a depressant

It's good that you're here, and we know that you're
    safe
We're a family, we're team mates, a crew
But we need our own space now, we haven't had sex
Since April 2002

You've got to grow up, kid, you live here rent-free
This we have got to discuss
We own a nice home, and a dog, and a car
So why can't you be more like us?

We married as teens, and then bought our first house
It even had its own grounds
We easily saved; why can't you do that?
(It only cost us eight pounds)

You save what you can, kid, we've both seen you try
To clamour your way out of debt
But we read an article saying that you
Spend all of your money in Pret

Your smile brings us joy, kid, your laugh makes us
   melt
Your tears bring us nothing but sorrow
That said, that's enough now, you've got to move out
Ideally as soon as tomorrow

It won't be like this for all time, kid, we're sure
Remember that you're in our will
You'll get the house back and your problems will fade
Just as soon as we're seriously ill

So let's go to sleep now, shut your eyes tight
And please don't you tremble or pout
Just have happy dreams, kid, like never before
Because, hey, tomorrow you're out

The Three Liberal Pigs

Once upon a time there were three liberal pigs, and a big bad wolf.

One day, the pigs were wallowing in their pen when they got word that the big bad wolf was on his way. Last time a big bad wolf got into the pen, it was carnage. The remaining pigs swore blind that such a tragedy would never befall them again.

'Let's build a house!' said the first pig. 'A strong, sturdy house that will keep the wolf away for good.'

'We need to build it together!' said the second pig. 'It's only by pooling our individual strengths and experiences that we can defeat such a powerful enemy. On our own we are nothing but lame ducks.'

'Hang on,' said the third pig, outraged. 'Did you just say "lame ducks"?'

'Yes I did,' said the second pig. 'For only unity in this matter will …'

'Lame ducks?' repeated the third pig. 'That's a bit problematic.'

'What?' said the second pig. 'Oh, no, you misunderstand. That's merely an expression. I don't have anything against ducks, disabled or otherwise.'

'It is a bit problematic, though,' said the first pig.

'Yeah, you're cancelled,' said the third pig.

'What?' shrieked the second pig. 'You can't cancel me! We're on the same team! Listen, the wolf is going to be here any minute! If we don't get our act together, he's going to eat us!'

'Hark at him,' said the third pig. 'Talk about a performative ally.'

'Woah, woah, woah,' shouted the first pig. 'What's with the "him" all of a sudden? We haven't established pronouns yet!'

'I do actually prefer them/their,' said the second pig.

'Shut it, performative ally,' shouted the third pig, now angrier at the other two pigs than he ever was at the wolf.

'Can we forget all this and start building the house?' said the second pig. 'The wolf will be here any minute.'

'Sure, fine, whatever,' said the third pig. 'What materials should we use?'

'I like straw,' said the first pig. 'It's locally sourced, it's sustainably produced, it's ...'

'It's going to get us bloody killed is what it's going to do,' said the second pig. 'Keeping out a wolf with straw? I've never heard anything so daft in all my life.'

'Oh yeah? Well, have you got any better ideas?' asked the first pig.

'Yeah,' said the second pig. 'Sticks.'

'STICKS?!' yelled the other two pigs in unison. 'What the hell sort of house are we going to build with sticks?'

'I appreciate that, but hear me out,' said the second pig. 'Straw is too flimsy, but rocks will take too long to gather. Sticks are a perfectly acceptable middle ground given the situation.'

'Classic bloody centrist,' huffed the third pig.

'I'm not a centrist,' said the second pig, hurt. 'In actual fact I'll have you know I'm a pragmatist.'

'Potato potahto,' said the third pig.

'Oh, mocking people with speech defects too now, are we?' huffed the first pig. 'You're bloody cancelled as well!'

This went on for some time. The pigs stood in the middle of their pen, screaming at each other for not perfectly fitting into their own narrow and ultra-specific world view until, eventually, the big bad wolf arrived.

Amused by all the infighting on display, the wolf sat down and watched. After twenty minutes or so of circular bickering, he interrupted the pigs just as pig two was in the middle of cancelling pig one for an insensitively worded tweet they wrote eight years ago.

'You aren't exactly doing yourselves any favours, you know,' said the wolf.

'Christ! It's the wolf!' cried the three pigs in unison.

'Look at you, squabbling among yourselves,' the wolf said. 'You'll never achieve any of your goals if you keep fighting each other like this.'

'But surely it's important to hold everyone to account for their wrongs, regardless of their overall beliefs,' said the third pig.

'Are you crazy?' said the wolf. 'Listen, the most important thing is power. You should overlook all these quibbles if they're keeping you from achieving power. Take me, for example. I can say anything I want and the other wolves will ignore it if it means we all get to eat pigs tonight.'

'Bollocks,' said pig one.

'It's true,' said the wolf. 'Watch this.'

The wolf raised himself up onto his hind legs, pointed his snout to the sky and yelled 'ALL THE DISABLED CHILDREN IN THE WORLD SHOULD BE THROWN IN A WELL!'

'Jesus Christ,' said the pigs. 'You can't say that!'

In the distance, two wolves looked up, rolled their eyes and carried on about their business.

'See?' said the wolf. 'But enough chit-chat. Because now, my dear pigs, it is time for you to become my dinner.'

The wolf smiled, revealing a set of sharp teeth. The wolf stretched, revealing all his sharp claws. He took one step towards the pigs. He – for some reason – ruffled his mop of blond hair in a motion that was clearly intended to be endearing. The pigs cowered in fear. Then suddenly a strange voice boomed out. Everyone turned around. It was another wolf.

'Wait! Wait!' the second wolf blustered, 'I want to be leader of the wolves!'

'You can't be the leader!' shouted the first wolf. 'You took drugs once! You admitted it.'

'Oh for god's sake', arguest the second wolf. 'We were all in the Oxford Union together. We *all* took drugs.'

'Especially me,' said a third wolf. 'Did I mention that I once smoked opium in Iran?'

'Shut up Rory,' snapped the first wolf.

'Don't tell him to shut up!' yelled the second wolf, 'I demand a species-wide referendum on your suitability as a leader'.

'Oh god,' wailed the first wolf. 'Anything but a referendum. Do you know how stupid it is to let people choose their own futures?'

'You're just scared of the televised debates,' said the second wolf.

'Treachery!' bellowed the first wolf. 'You've always had it in for me, ever since we shared a house at Eton!'

Then the second wolf wailed 'BULLER, BULLER, BULLER!' and lunged at the first wolf, biting and scratching him while the third wolf tore into both of them indiscriminately.

And, in this moment, the pigs felt a brand-new sensation. They felt self-aware.

'God, is this what *we* sound like?' asked pig three.

'I think it is,' replied pig one. 'Guys, I'm sorry. I can see now how petty we've been. We've blinded ourselves from our true cause with all these stupid distractions.'

'We can learn from this,' added pig two. 'There's still time for us to work together. Let's leg it!'

So, as the wolves continued to fight each other, the three pigs ran away as fast as their hooves could carry them. They built a house, made of a secure straw/stick/stone composite, learned to resolve their differences through respectful dialogue, and the wolf never troubled them again.

The Hare and the Tortoise
and the Russians

Once upon a time, in a field near a forest, there lived a happy hare and a sleepy tortoise. All day long the hare sprinted in circles around the tortoise until the tortoise became dizzy.

'I'm the fastest animal in the field!' bragged the hare to the tortoise. 'I'm faster than a fox, I'm faster than a cheetah, and I'm certainly faster than you!'

'Oh, please be quiet,' said the tortoise, slowly and quietly. 'I'm getting sick of all your boasting.'

'I won't be quiet!' shouted the hare. 'I'm faster than you! I'm faster than you!'

'Fine,' said the tortoise. 'Let's settle this once and for all. Let's race tomorrow.' The hare, knowing that he could never lose, agreed.

Tomorrow came, and all the animals gathered in the field to cheer on the hare. They knew that the tortoise would never win. He was too slow and the hare was too fast. It physically couldn't be done.

A hush fell across the field. It was time to start. 'Three, two, one, go!' hooted an owl, and the race was on.

Straight away, the hare shot off into the distance, leaving a trail of dust in his wake. Meanwhile, the tortoise carefully and deliberately put one foot in front of the other. Within seconds, an impossible gap had opened up.

The hare looked behind him, and saw that the tortoise was nowhere to be seen. 'I'm so far ahead,' he thought. 'Maybe I'll just have a little nap underneath this tree. He won't catch me.'

So the hare curled up in a warm little ball in the shade of the tree, and went to sleep.

He woke up to the sound of distant cheering. 'What's going on?' he thought. Quick as a flash he ran to the finish line, only to see the tortoise standing there with a medal around his neck.

'This can't be right!' shouted the hare. 'I'm much faster than the stupid tortoise! He must have cheated!'

'I didn't cheat,' said the tortoise. 'You fell asleep under that tree and I simply plodded on past you. Slow and steady always wins.'

'But that doesn't make sense,' argued the hare. 'I was so far ahead of you that I could have slept for six hours and still beaten you.'

'You lost,' snapped the tortoise. 'Get over it.'

Dejected, the hare walked home to sleep off his defeat. But still ... something didn't sit right with him. He was a hare, for crying out loud. Hares are much faster than tortoises. Everyone knows that. Ask anyone what the defining characteristic of a tortoise is and they're going to say 'slow'. Guaranteed. Perhaps 'shell', but probably 'slow'.

So the hare spent all night pinning photos to his bedroom wall, and connecting them all with string. He had to find out how the slow tortoise managed to beat him. He had to, even if it killed him.

After three days and three nights the exhausted and frazzled hare had an epiphany. He climbed out of his burrow and staggered to the tortoise's house, alarming passers-by with his unwashed stench. When he arrived, he banged on the tortoise's door, loud enough for the whole field to hear.

'Tortoise!' he shouted. 'You're being funded by the Russians!'

Three minutes later, the tortoise opened the door. Clearly, this was important.

'I beat you fair and square! I'm the people's tortoise!' yelled the tortoise.

'Oh yeah?' shouted the hare. 'Then how do you explain THESE?'

With a flourish, the hare banged on the wall of the tortoise's house, causing a hidden door to flip open. Inside the door were a gleaming pair of shiny chrome jet skates.

All the animals in the field gasped.

'So what?' said the tortoise. 'I've got jet skates. Jet skates don't prove anything.'

'Then what does THIS say?' said the hare, pointing to an inscription on the heel of the skates reading 'отправлено с любовью от великого лидера'.

'That's the brand name!' protested the tortoise.

'The brand name is With Love From The Great Leader?' asked the hare incredulously. 'I put it to you, tortoise, that slow and steady doesn't always win at all. It's colluding with the Russians that wins.'

'No collusion!' shouted the tortoise, and slammed his door.

The hare was on to something, he knew it. For days and nights he fastidiously picked apart every last thread of the case and carefully followed it back until a larger picture emerged. Once it did, he returned to the tortoise's house. The tortoise was waiting for him, surrounded by his menacing tortoise children and faceless corporate tortoise legal team.

'Well here he is,' shouted the tortoise, 'Crooked Hare.'

'Crooked Hare?' replied the hare. 'But crookedness is exactly what I'm accusing you of.'

'This is a witch-hunt!' shouted the tortoise.

'Sir, I promise you that this is not a witch-hunt,' replied the hare, as calmly as he could. 'I know the truth, OK?'

'What truth is that, Crooked Hare?' bellowed the tortoise.

'The Kompromat,' explained the hare.

Slowly and clearly, so that everyone could hear, the hare explained that the Russian government had spent a fortune over the years on intelligence designed to destabilise as many foreign fields as it could. After all, now that all the animals believed that a tortoise could beat a hare in a foot race, they were more liable to swallow all manner of anti-field propaganda.

'Destabilisation?' crowed the tortoise. 'Where's your proof?'

'Remember last month by the lake, when a hen flew faster than a duck? Remember Old McGregor's farm, when a mouse beat a cow in a boxing match? It all makes so much sense now. It's the Russians. It has to be the Russians!'

'It isn't the Russians!' shouted the tortoise.

'It is!' shouted the hare.

'Covfefe!' shouted the tortoise.

'What?' shouted the hare.

'Fine, it was us,' said a thick-accented figure behind the tortoise's door. It opened, and there stood none other than Vladimir Putin.

Vladimir Putin said that, since the hare had figured it all out, he may as well own up to his shenanigans. Several years ago, he said, he invited the tortoise to Moscow. He wined and dined him like never before and, in the evening, provided him with the services of dozens of high-class tortoise sex workers.

The tortoise had made the sex workers urinate all over a photo of the hare, much to his obvious gratification. But what the tortoise didn't know was that this was all being secretly filmed by the Russian government to be used as a blackmail tool at a later date.

Soon, riddled with shame, the tortoise had no choice but to carry out Putin's wishes, feeding a slow and toxic stream of misinformation about Putin's rivals into the field. The race marked the second phase of Putin's plan, but neither Putin nor the tortoise had assumed that the hare would make such a diligent detective.

'It's all over now!' laughed the hare upon hearing the truth.

'No it isn't,' replied Putin. He then explained that the mainstream media now operated on a such a fast-twitch high-frequency degree of panic that, even if the story of the tortoise's collusion was made public, he'd just get the tortoise to say something weird or tweet something silly, and the resulting mess would push the collusion out of the news cycle within minutes. 'You lost, Comrade Hare,' laughed Putin.

'Not this time, buster,' said the hare. 'This time, we're going to do the right thing.'

So, instead of resorting to the instant gratification of a quick public takedown, the hare organised a small grassroots movement that expressly promoted the ideas of fairness and tolerance. It was hard work, but the hare gradually convinced all the animals to focus on the core ideals that had made the field such a wide-spread beacon for good all those years ago. Soon the animals realised that it takes sustained effort to maintain a functioning field, and they all committed to playing their part, and before long they were educated and energised. And Putin failed because nothing, not even a wealthy foreign influence fixing the outcome of races for its private gain, can thrive in the face of an educated and energised population.

The moral of this story is simple: all tortoises are bastards.

Jack and the Sustainably Produced Meat-Substitute Stalk

Once upon a time, an old widow lived on a farm with her son Jack. Every day, Jack would help his mother with the chores; slaughtering the chickens, lethally stunning the cows, grinding up all the goats into an unidentifiable sludge. But despite all their hard work, Jack and his mother were very poor.

'What shall we do?' worried the widow one morning. 'We don't have enough money to buy the mechanically-operated bolt guns needed to kill all our cows. We must sell our pet dog Old Bella at market, and with the money we can buy our murder gun.'

'OK mother,' replied Jack. 'Today is market day, so I will go and sell Old Bella.'

So Jack took Old Bella's lead in his hand and walked off to market. Just as he passed the garden gate, he saw a strange old man smiling at him.

'Hello Jack,' said the man.

'How do you know my name?' Jack asked.

'Tell me, Jack,' said the old man mysteriously. 'What are you doing today?'

'Why, I'm taking my dog to market,' replied Jack.

'But market is such a long way away,' said the old man. 'Here, perhaps I can help you. Let's do a trade. I'll take your dog and spare you the journey to market, and in return you can have these.'

The old man looked around to make sure nobody was looking, and then opened his palm. Inside his hand were three small cubes of silken tofu.

'What is this?' asked Jack.

'It's magic tofu. Would you like to know what magic tofu does? It is an excellent source of amino acids, iron, calcium and other ...'

'Thanks mister!' shouted Jack, as he swiped the tofu from the old man's hand.

'But I haven't finished explaining the benefits of ...'

'Bye!' yelled Jack, as he threw Old Bella's lead into the old man's face and ran home.

Jack's mother grinned as Jack returned. 'My wonderful boy,' she cried. 'Pray tell, how much money did you make from selling Old Bella at market?'

Jack smiled and reached into his pocket. 'I got something even more precious than money, dear mother. Look, this is ...'

'Is that TOFU?!' screamed his mother in horror.

'It is, mother', replied Jack. 'Nutritionists claim that it's a complete source of protei...'

'How dare you!' raged his mother. 'No son of mine is going to eat tofu. I've seen this happen before. It starts with tofu, then it becomes an interest in contemporary dance, and before you know it you're running a homeopathic crystal pop-up in Hackney Wick.'

'That's a weirdly intense escalation,' stammered Jack, bemused, but it was too late. Jack's mother grabbed the tofu cubes from Jack's hand and flung them out of the window.

'Now, you'll eat this plate of dead goat and go to bed,' she roared.

When Jack woke the next morning, he drew back his curtains and saw something incredible. Why, the tofu had sprouted overnight and grown into an almighty tofu stalk that stretched up through the clouds.

Curious, Jack climbed and climbed the stalk until at last he reached the sky. And when he got there he found a long road winding its way through the clouds to a mighty castle in the distance.

Jack ran along the road but, just as he reached the castle, he saw a terrible giant loom into the horizon, sniffing the air hungrily. Jack watched as the giant shouted a terrible rhyme:

Fee-fi-fo-fubstitute
I smell a whiff of a sustainably produced meat
  substitute.

Jack was frightened. He tried to hide behind a cloud, but it was too late. The giant clapped his terrible eyes on Jack. With one swift movement, he picked the boy up and held him to his face. Jack winced, for the giant's breath reeked of edamame beans.

'You, boy!' roared the giant. 'What are you doing here?'

'Please don't eat me!' cowered Jack, fearful for his life. 'I'm just a simple farmer boy. I mean no harm.'

'Eat you?' replied the giant. 'Why would I eat you? You're made of meat, aren't you? Yuck! I'm not a barbarian.' Jack spied a copy of the Extinction Rebellion handbook poking from the top of the giant's waistcoat which, now he thought of it, looked suspiciously like it was made of reclaimed fabric and might have been produced by ethically-accredited woman's collective in India.

'Then what do you want with me?' stammered Jack.

'Got any facon?'

'Facon?'

'Facon. Fake bacon.'

'Sir,' replied Jack, 'I must profess that I do not.'

'What then?' shouted the giant. 'Quorn? Mock duck? Tofurkey? A nice Linda McCartney sausage? I could murder a nice Linda McCartney sausage.'

'Kind giant, I cannot help you,' said Jack. 'I am but a simple boy from a simple meat farm, and ...'

'Meat farm?' replied the giant. 'Yuck! Do you know how barbaric human consumption of meat is?'

'Alas kind giant, I do not,' said Jack.

'Right, wait there,' said the giant, putting Jack back down, 'I've got *Cowspiracy* on DVD back at the castle. Have you watched it? I simply couldn't justify eating meat after I saw the conditions those poor cows were kept in.'

But as the giant ran back to his castle to arm himself with pro-vegan paraphernalia, Jack saw his chance for escape. Quick as a flash, he ran back towards the stalk and began his descent down to the farm. He hadn't got far, though, when the giant returned.

'I've also printed off some recipes for jackfruit curry that I think you might also ... hey!' called the giant as he saw his new friend vanish below the clouds. 'Come back here!'

Scared of this newfound alternative lifestyle for reasons he couldn't quite vocalise, Jack pelted down the stalk as fast as he could. But the giant was hot on his tail.

'Just come back here for a second,' yelled the giant as he clambered down the stalk. 'It's fine if you're not into it, but you could at least arm yourself with the best possible information.'

Just then, the giant slipped. His giant hands let go of the stalk, and his giant body plummeted to the ground below. Just before he crashed to earth with an almighty smack, he called out to Jack 'Think of the CO_2 emissions!'

The crash of the giant woke Jack's mother. She ran to the front door in her nightgown just as Jack was climbing off the stalk.

'You foolish boy!' she cried. 'What have you done? We're ruined! Ruined!'

But just then, a giant ball rolled out of the giant's giant pocket. It was the size of five cows, and it smelled delicious.

'What's this?' enquired Jack's mother, breaking off a chunk and eating it. 'This is ... this is ... is this soy pulp? It's incredible.'

Jack scooped some up on his finger and tasted it too. 'Wow!' he exclaimed. 'This is so much better than meat. What an ethical and versatile source of protein!'

'Jack,' sobbed his mother, 'You've saved us. You've saved us all. Go and set the cows free. Go and burn the chicken slaughter machine. We have no need to live off animal flesh any longer. Your huge dead friend has taught me the errors of my ways!'

'Yeah, about that,' replied Jack. 'Do you think the giant has any family we should contact, or ...'

'Don't be silly,' cried his mother. 'We have soy pulp to eat!'

Jack and his mother danced in celebration, and they all lived happily ever after.

The Man Who Couldn't Even Hug Anyone Any More

Once upon a time there was a man who couldn't even hug anybody any more. One day, the man's niece came to visit him.

At the airport, the niece spread her arms wide as she ran to greet him. 'Uncle, Uncle!' she cried. 'I have not seen you for many years, and I have missed you so much. I have so many things to tell you, my favourite uncle! Please, hug me like you did when I was a little girl!'

The man flinched and stepped aside. 'Are you KIDDING?' he yelled, cowering behind a pillar. 'Hug you? In an airport? In front of all these people? What are you, nuts?'

The man's niece was confused. 'But Uncle,' she cried, 'when I was younger, you would hug me every day. You used to give me piggybacks around your garden and throw me high in the air! Please, Uncle, hug me like you did in the old days!'

'Not bloody likely,' said the man, as he gingerly extended a consent form stating that his niece explicitly consented to a brief, business-like handshake.

As he drove his niece home, the man saw a broken-down car on the side of the road. Bent under the bonnet was a woman. She was crying.

The man pulled over and got out. 'Hello, what seems to be the problem here?' he asked the woman.

'It's my car!' the woman sobbed. 'I was driving along, and then the engine just stopped. Oh, I am so far from home, and I have no money to pay for a mechanic. Whatever should I do?'

The man looked at the engine. 'I think I can see what the problem is,' he told the woman. So he rolled up his sleeves and fiddled with her engine for a minute or two.

'There, try that,' said the man when he was finished.

The woman turned the key in the ignition, and the car started perfectly. The woman was overjoyed. She got out of the car and ran over to the man.

'Thank you! Oh, thank you!' she cried. 'Now I can drive home and see my family again! Oh, thank you so much.' She spread her arms wide for a hug, and the man ran away.

'Nice try!' he shouted. 'I know your game, but I'm not going to be arrested! Not today!'

The man jumped in his car and drove away as fast as he could, leaving the woman scratching her head in the distance.

The man arrived home. As his niece retrieved her luggage from the boot, the front door of his house burst wide open. Two small children came running out, their faces a picture of uncontrolled delight.

'Daddy! Daddy!' they yelled in unison, hardly able to believe that their beloved father had finally returned to them. 'Oh Daddy, we missed you so much!' They leapt into the air as one, soaring through the sky with their arms stretched wide so that their father could catch them.

'WOAH!' yelled the man as he ran for cover, letting his children crash to the ground with a sickening thud.

'What the hell is going on here?' shouted the man's wife, drawn outside by the commotion and confronted with the sight of her children lying screaming in the middle of the road.

'Phew, talk about a close shave!' said the man. 'I could have been ruined if they'd managed to latch on. Ruined!'

'Keith, they're your children,' said his wife. 'They were just pleased to see you.'

'Don't you understand?' said the man, 'You can't even hug anyone any more.'

'I think you can, Uncle Keith,' said the niece. 'I think it's just that ...'

'No you can't!' interrupted the man. 'You absolutely can't. My colleague Ian was fired last week because he hugged someone. Ask anyone.'

'He wasn't fired for hugging,' sighed his wife. 'He was fired for systematically harassing a woman fifteen years his junior.'

'Same thing!' shouted the man.

'It's not really the same thing at all,' said his niece.

'Yes it is!' shouted the man. 'I read an article about it in the *Daily Telegraph*! It said that middle-aged white men are being persecuted for showing affection, and as such they are the last true minority in this country.'

'Wow,' said his wife.

'Daddy, Daddy, why did you let us hurt ourselves like that?' cried the man's injured children as they limped towards him on broken ankles.

'Get away! Get away from me you demons! I saw what people like you did to Donald Trump!' shouted the man.

'Donald Trump didn't hug anyone, you idiot,' said Jane, Keith's wife. 'He literally bragged about grabbing women's genitalia.'

'And he wasn't fired either,' said his niece. 'They let him be president of America.'

Jane was concerned. 'Are you OK, Keith?' she asked, putting her hand on his shoulder. 'Did you bang your head?'

'GET YOUR HAND OFF MY SHOULDER, WOMAN!' the man screamed. 'DON'T YOU DARE #METOO ME FOR THIS! I'M A MARRIED MAN!'

So the man ran into the house and up the stairs and into his bedroom, where he clambered into an elaborate plastic sterile containment bubble that he bought from a retired immunodeficiency doctor on eBay.

And there he stayed for the rest of his life, sufficiently convinced that he had won the war on middle-aged white men that had only ever existed inside his own head.

Great Pacific Garbage Patch

The Great Pacific Garbage Patch woke up one morning and stretched. As he stretched, all 80,000 tonnes of him twisted and turned in the warmth of the ocean. He looked to his left, and saw Japan. He looked to his right, and saw California. As usual, there was nothing else around him. He sighed. Another day alone.

True, he'd heard of the other great polluted subtropical gyres that burbled away on other parts of the planet. He'd heard of the Indian Ocean Garbage Patch, massive enough to trick locals into thinking that it was actually the remnants of a downed passenger jet. He'd heard of the North Atlantic Garbage Patch, too; a comparative minnow that nevertheless managed to poison scores of fish with its brave dedication to the relentless production of microplastics.

He'd heard of them, but he'd never met them. For

he knew that if they ever were to meet, they would simply be absorbed into his orbit, and then he'd be alone once more. Oh, how the Great Pacific Garbage Patch longed for company.

But it wasn't to be. He was resigned to that now. He knew that every friendship he ever made was doomed. The turtles he tried to befriend ended up getting tangled in all his discarded fishing nets. The seagulls he tried to befriend all choked on used condoms and decayed into little beaky skeletons. He even tried making friends with a sperm whale once, but then the whale ingested 65lb of plastic bags and rope and glass, and its abdomen became infected, and it died and washed up on a beach, and a local marine organisation tweeted a photo of the contents of his stomach. All in all, the Garbage Patch determined, it wasn't exactly an ideal first date.

So the Great Pacific Garbage Patch had nothing to do but drift. Day after day he'd aimlessly drift through the ocean, like the saddest colossal floating island of poisonous detritus you've ever seen. All he could do was toxify enough of the food chain to eventually destroy mankind, but that wouldn't happen for twenty or thirty years at least. He may as well just give up, he thought.

But just then something magical happened. From the sky drifted a miraculous sight; a blue fairy, no bigger than Hawaii. She gazed upon this melancholy trash island, millions of square miles in size, and cooed at him soothingly.

'Great Pacific Garbage Patch, you looked troubled,' she said.

'Blue Fairy, I am miserable,' the patch replied. 'I'm so lonely. I kill everything I touch. I'm like King Midas, if that story was about a guy who basically just exploded dolphins with sludge.'

'Great Pacific Garbage Patch,' the Fairy said, 'I can do something to ease your pain. I am the answer to your prayers, for I have the power to transform you.'

'Into what?' asked the patch.

'That is your decision, and your decision alone', she warned. 'However, may I suggest transforming you into thousands of square miles of Antarctic sheet ice, in order to counteract the effects of climate cha ...'

'I want to be a real boy!' blurted the patch.

'Huh?' said the Blue Fairy.

'Yeah! A real boy!' shouted the patch. 'You did it to that Italian puppet, so you can do it to me.'

'But from an ecological perspective, perhaps it would be better if ...'

'Is this my wish or yours?' demanded the garbage patch, who was turning out to be quite a diva.

'I mean it's yours, but ...'

'Well then, make me a real boy', said the patch. 'I could grow up to become a renowned environmental activist, spreading the word about the state of the world until mankind takes responsibility for its actions, working together to build a sustainable future for generations to come.'

'Fine,' muttered the Blue Fairy. 'I'll transform you into a real boy, but to help your ecological journey, I shall assign you an official conscience. Now go forth, Great Pacific Garbage Patch, and be noble.'

With that, the Blue Fairy clicked her fingers and disappeared in a puff of smoke.

* * *

A boy woke up and stretched. As he stretched, his arms and legs barely reached the ends of his bed. He had a bed! He had arms and legs! He looked to his left, and saw his bedroom wall lovingly decorated with pictures of his family. He had a home! He had a family! He wasn't an island of floating rubbish anymore! He was a real boy!

'Howdy partner!' called a small voice next to him.

The boy looked over at his bedside cabinet and saw a terrapin standing there in a top hat.

'Who are you?' asked the boy.

'Why it's me', replied the terrapin. 'It's your old pal Jurtley Turtle. I'm your conscience! The Blue Fairy hired me to keep you on the straight and narrow!'

'Conscience,' the boy said, 'I am so comfortable. What is this thing that I lie upon?'

'That's called a mattress', the terrapin replied.

'What is it made from, conscience?' he asked. 'Is it sustainable?'

'Why, I hate to tell you,' said the Terrapin, 'but it's a mixture of petroleum-based polyurethane foam, for-maldehyde, toxic flame retardants and boric acid. The likelihood is that it'll spend hundreds of years taking up space in a landfill when you're done with it.'

The boy paused.

'Comfortable, though, isn't it?' he said.

Jurtley Turtle narrowed his eyes. Then he said 'Hey, you're a real boy now, and real boys can't just stay in bed all day. It's time to get up and go to school!'

The boy looked out of his bedroom window and saw that it was raining. 'I don't really want to walk in the rain,' he said. 'Maybe I'll get an Uber.'

'Wait!' shouted the terrapin. 'Even if your taxi is electric – which, in itself, is vastly unlikely – its heavy battery will increase wear on the tyres, which will in turn increase its emissions of rubber particulate matter far beyond the minimum safe level.'

The boy stared at the terrapin. Then he sighed and pulled out his phone.

'A PHONE?!' the terrapin cried, aghast. 'Oh boy, those things are really bad news! They're made from materials that have to be mined from the Earth at enormous cost, so their carbon footprint is catastrophic. Plus you'll want to replace it in a couple of years, which produces an extraordinary level of waste. And, don't get me started on how much fossil fuel gets burned by the data centres that run all your cloud-based applications ...'

The boy grabbed a jam jar from his bedside cabinet. 'Conscience, can you do me a favour and hop in here for a second?' he asked.

Sure I can!" replied Jurtley Turtle, climbing inside. 'I love reusable jars. Although, you know, the industrial jam industry isn't exactly a picture of virtue, because ...'

As the terrapin continued his terrible warnings about Big Jam, the boy silently screwed a lid on the jar, put it in his pyjama pocket and went downstairs. In the kitchen, he opened his fridge and pulled out a chilled bottle of Evian.

'BOTTLED WATER?!' screamed Jurtley Turtle, muffled through the glass. 'You have a perfectly good tap RIGHT THERE! Oh god! Oh no! You're killing the planet. You're killing it!'

So, the boy put the jar in a drawer and calmly went about his business, trying and failing to do his best in a world of easily compromised ideals. But at least there wasn't a massive trash island in the sea anymore, so that's something.

Hansel and Gretel,
the Two Arseholes

Near a great dark forest there lived a poor woodcutter and his twins, a boy named Hansel and a girl named Gretel. Their mother had died shortly after childbirth, and the woodcutter had since remarried. His new wife was a cruel woman; grasping and needy and constantly desperate for the woodcutter's attention.

One day a great famine came, and the woodcutter worried about providing enough food. 'What is to become of us?' he asked his wife in vain. 'How can we feed our children when we have nothing for ourselves?'

His wife had an idea. 'It's impossible,' she told him, 'So this is what we will do. Early tomorrow morning we will take Hansel and Gretel into the deepest, darkest part of the forest and build a fire. While they are attending to the fire, we will slip away and they will never find their way back. Finally we will be rid of them.'

Hansel and Gretel, too hungry to sleep, overheard this entire conversation. Gretel cried bitter tears at their father's betrayal. 'Our stepmother is a wicked woman,' she wailed. 'She wants us dead so she can have him all to herself.'

'Fear not, sister,' said Hansel. 'Please sleep, for I know exactly what to do.'

Late that night, when everyone was sleeping, Hansel got dressed, snuck into the kitchen and filled his pockets with the last remaining scraps of bread.

The next morning their stepmother awoke them. 'Wake up you ungrateful children!' she shouted. 'We have no firewood. It's time to collect some from the forest.'

'We hate you!' shouted Hansel in response. 'We've always hated you!'

But, nevertheless, all four of them set out into the woods. As they walked, Hansel quietly picked off pieces of bread and dropped them on the floor, creating a small trail of breadcrumbs to show him the way back to their cottage.

Once they had reached the deepest, darkest part of the forest, the woodcutter built a fire for his children. 'This has been a long and tiring walk,' he said. 'You two rest here, and we will return once we have collected enough firewood.' With that, he and his wife left.

Hours passed, but the woodcutter did not return. Night fell, and Gretel began to cry. 'We're lost, Hansel!' she sobbed. 'Our father has abandoned us and we are lost in the forest!'

'Fear not, sister,' said Hansel. 'I left a trail of bread-crumbs from the cottage. We can easily find our way home. All we have to do is follow the bread.'

But they could not follow the bread, for the bread-crumbs had been eaten by the birds and animals of the forest. Gretel began to cry once more, for she knew that all hope was lost, but Hansel was brave. 'Fear not, sister,' he said once more. 'We will find our way home.'

Hansel and Gretel walked through the night, and through the next day, and into the night again, but they could not find their way home. Deeper and darker into the forest they went, farther than they had ever been, until they found themselves scared and lost and hungry.

But then, through a crack in the trees, they saw a house. It was a strange house, made entirely of gin-gerbread and cake. 'This is our salvation, sister,' whis-pered Hansel triumphantly. 'We can break off enough of this house to fill our pockets, and then eat it while we find our way home.'

Hansel reached up and tore a piece from the roof. 'Should we be doing this?' asked Gretel. 'Of course we should, sister,' replied Hansel. 'We'll need food if we are to make our way back to Father.'

But as he kept ripping pieces from the house, Hansel failed to notice that a gruesome witch was standing behind them. The witch was as old as the hills; gnarled and wizened. She had warts on her nose and her hair was grey. She was hideous to look at, and she spoke in a terrifying croak.

'Stop it!' shouted the witch. 'You two wicked children are destroying my house!'

'Forgive us,' pleaded Gretel. 'We are lost and hungry, and we only wish to find our father. We are so terribly sorry about your house.'

'You're lost?' asked the witch. 'You're alone? Oh, you poor things. Please, please, come into the house. I will cook you a proper meal, and you can sleep on my spare bed, and tomorrow we will all go and find your father together.'

Hansel was suspicious, but too tired to argue. They followed the witch into the house, and sat down in the kitchen. 'I have to start my oven,' she told the children. 'It's a big oven, large enough to cook two small pigs.'

Hansel looked at Gretel, then back at himself, then at the oven. They could both fit inside, he realised.

'Look at the state of you,' the witch continued.

'You're too thin! You two need to be fattened up good and proper.' Then she licked her lips.

Hansel's eyes widened in horror. Without thinking he stood up and pushed the witch hard, knocking her head against the oven door. The witch fell to the floor in agony.

'You will not eat us, witch!' he shouted.

'What?' replied the witch. 'Who's a witch?'

'You are!' shouted Hansel. 'I know a witch when I see one!'

'I think you are mistaken, child,' replied the witch. 'I am just a simple old woman.'

'Oh yeah? Then where's your husband?' asked Hansel.

'I never married,' said the witch.

'Because you're a WITCH!' bellowed Hansel.

The witch was flummoxed. 'No, not because I'm a witch; because I never saw the point of getting married. I've always thought it was slightly archaic to commit to one partner for your entire life, to be honest.'

'Tell me, witch,' shouted Hansel, 'If you're not a witch, then why do you live so deep in the forest?'

'I don't live here, you idiot,' the witch replied. 'I'm an artist. The Forestry Commission contracted me to build a structural artwork demonstrating the fragile nature of the food chain. Honestly, what sort of a weirdo would live in a house made of cake?'

'If you don't live here, witch, then why are you here tonight?' asked Hansel.

'To start the oven,' replied the witch. 'I needed to dry out some of the gingerbread on the roof. As soon as it was alight, I was going to drive home to my flat. I was going to take you with me. That's where my spare bed is.'

Hansel closed his eyes tight, trying to comprehend exactly what was going on.

'Hold on a minute,' said the witch. 'Did you think I was a witch just because I'm an unmarried woman of a certain age? Is that your automatic go-to in situations like this?'

'Yes,' mumbled Hansel.

'Jesus Christ, kid, your whole value system is terrible,' replied the witch, who was actually a well-regarded conceptual artist called Judith Miller OBE.

'Please,' cried Gretel through a veil of tears. 'You have to help us. Our father is married to an evil woman.'

'Really?' replied the witch. 'Why is she evil?'

'Because she isn't our mother!' yelled Hansel, defiant.

'Did she kill your mother?' asked the witch.

'No, but she married our father after Mother died.'

'So you hate her because she allowed your father to

move on from a period of what sounds like devastating personal grief?'

'No!' shouted Hansel. 'We hate her because she hates children.'

'How do you know she hates children?' asked the witch.

'Because she doesn't have any of her own!' shouted Hansel.

'That doesn't make her evil, you weird little bastard!' replied the witch. 'Maybe she isn't able to have children. Maybe she just never wanted children. Maybe she loves your father so much that she put her own personal ambitions to one side in order to raise the family he already had. Did you ever think of any of that, you massive arsehole?'

'But she left us in the forest,' sobbed Gretel.

'I'd fucking leave you in the forest if you kept calling me evil all your life,' replied the witch. 'Oh and by the way, Gretel, literally all you've done this entire story is cry. Where's your sense of agency? You've just let your brother make all the decisions, and he's an enormous dickhead.'

'Well now, wait a minute,' began Hansel.

'You left a trail of breadcrumbs, you moron,' said the witch. 'Breadcrumbs! In a forest. Of course they're all going to be eaten. Hey, you know what you could have used that wouldn't have been eaten?'

'No,' replied Hansel.

'LITERALLY ANYTHING THAT WASN'T BREAD,' shouted the witch.

'Oh yeah,' mumbled Hansel.

'I'm not supposed to make decisions, anyway,' said Gretel. 'Father says that women are for cooking and cleaning and looking pretty and nothing else.'

'*WHAT*?' shouted the witch. 'Where did he hear *that*?'

'On Reddit,' replied Gretel. 'He's a men's rights activist.'

'OK, I've heard enough of this,' huffed the witch. So she packed Hansel and Gretel up in her car, and drove them to her comfortable flat in the city. And then she spent the rest of her life raising them as her own in an open and non-judgemental environment, watching them slowly blossom into conscientious young adults who refused to adhere to society's toxic gender roles. They were happy and empathetic, and the witch was proud of them.

And they all lived happily ever after, except for the woodcutter who just sat around downvoting YouTube trailers for any films with female leads until his wife left him.

Trumplestiltskin

Once upon a time there was a miller who had a daughter. A beautiful daughter. People said she was the most beautiful daughter you've ever seen. I mean, she was a total knockout; a real ten, that one. If I weren't the narrator, I'd want to kiss her. I would. I would.

Now, this miller was a real loser. A real loser. It was a shame. He went to visit the king – who is a great friend of mine, does a wonderful job, great guy – and he said, 'My daughter can spin gold out of straw'. She couldn't. Total fake news.

The king believed this guy, though. Lyin' Miller, I called him. So Lyin' Miller said 'My daughter can spin gold out of straw,' and the king – a terrific man in many ways – said, 'Great, bring her to my palace tomorrow.' And that was smart of him. Really, it was. Because if she can spin gold out of straw, that's great.

Lots of gold for everyone. But if she can't, he's got a pretty girl locked up in his palace forever. And I'm not saying he'd do anything to her. I'm not. If I was the king, who knows, but I'm not. I'm just the narrator. That's all.

So the next morning, Lyin' Miller brings his daughter to the king's palace – beautiful place, very nice – and she gets taken to a room filled with straw. 'What am I doing here?' she asks, and the king says, 'Your fat pig of a father told me you could spin gold out of straw.'

Listen, you should have seen her face, I'm telling you. She was all 'No, no, no,' and 'My dad's a gross old phony', but it was too late. The king wanted gold, so he gave her a spinning wheel and said that he'd kill her if she hadn't spun any gold by the next morning. A good man, the king. Very, very tough. Sometimes you've got to be tough, you know? Gotta be tough.

The daughter sat down on the straw and cried. 'My father is frankly a huge disgrace,' she whined. 'I might be just about the hottest thing anyone has ever seen, but I can't work magic. Oh no, I'm gonna get killed. What a waste of this beautiful body.'

But then this little guy walked in. Strange little guy, very small, weird looking guy. I don't like to talk this way about people, you know, but you brought it up. I don't bring it up. I could say I have no comment on how he looked, but that's not me. Ugly. He was ugly. Grotesque. But you shouldn't have brought it up. It's your fault.

This guy said, 'Why are you crying?' and the daughter said, 'I have to spin straw into gold or else I'll be killed, but I don't know how to spin straw into gold'. The guy said 'Why not?' and the daughter said 'Because I'm only fifteen years old'. I mentioned that she was only fifteen, right? No? I meant to.

This put the guy in a really terrific bargaining position, because he held all the cards at this point. Very, very smart. He waited until he had all the cards. 'What will you give me if I spin straw into gold for you?' he asked.

'I have nothing to give you,' she said. 'I have no possessions in the whole entire world, because my father is a fat loser.'

'Then give me that ring on your finger', said the guy. This was very smart, because she had no choice. All the cards. Very smart.

So, the daughter gave the guy her ring, and the guy sat down at the spinning wheel, and he started spinning gold. The girl was blown away. She'd never seen anything like it. Nobody had. Unbelievable.

Now, a stupid guy would have spun all the straw into gold right there and then, but not this guy. He was a real high-quality guy, a great negotiator. He filled two bobbins with gold, said goodbye and then walked off with the ring.

The next day, the king – very nice man, very smart, pretty good golfer, not as good as me – came in and saw the gold. 'Great, good, OK', he said, 'But where's the rest?'

'What do you mean, the rest?' said the daughter. She was beautiful – very sexy, very hot, fifteen-years-old – but maybe not the smartest. The king said 'Make me more gold, or I'll chop you up and feed you to my pigs.' And sometimes that's how you've got to be, OK? It's nothing personal. It's just business.

So again the daughter started crying and crying. It was embarrassing, quite frankly. But then the guy showed up again. Very smart. Not as smart as me, but very smart. 'What will you give me if I turn the rest into gold?' he said.

'I don't have anything,' she replied. 'You already took my ring; which, by the way, is a very bad ring, not good quality, it sucks, my fat, dumb, loser dad gave it to me, it's a shame.'

'Then I'll marry you,' said the guy.

The daughter didn't want to get married to the guy, because he was gross. So ugly. The worst. I hate bringing it up, but you asked me about him. She could do so much better than him – she could stay in all night and kiss a handsome narrator on the lips like a good girl maybe – but she didn't have a choice. He held all the cards. Very smart. So what could she do? She agreed to marry him.·

The guy sat at the spinning wheel and span gold all through the night. It was incredible. By morning the room was totally covered in gold. The place looked spectacular, like how a poor person would imagine a rich person's house. Very, very classy.

The king saw all the gold, and he was very happy. Very happy. 'Look at all this gold!' he said. 'I could make something real classy with this, like a toilet paper holder shaped like a swan.' And he let her go, which was a bad move if you ask me because there's always more straw, you know? It isn't what I would have done. The king was a nice guy. Maybe too nice. Who knows? I don't know.

So the daughter goes home to her fat, lazy father, and she says 'Hey, Lyin' Miller! How could you do this to me?' and she shoots him, and he dies, and maybe it's a good thing. It's not pretty, you know, but now he's out of the picture so everyone's happy.

Happy ever after, right? Wrong, because then the weird-looking guy came back again. 'Remember you said we'd get married?' he said to the daughter, and the daughter started crying again, and that was a shame because crying made her much less sexy. The guy looked at her, face all ugly and scrunched up, and he thinks 'Wow, this girl's only a six when she cries,' so he tries to back out of the deal by asking her an impossible question. Sensible guy. Maybe he could marry someone younger and less emotional instead. Who knows?

'Listen,' he says. 'I know I said I'd marry you – and I still could marry you, because we had an agreement, remember? There's nothing in the law to stop me from marrying you – but if you can guess my name, I'll let you go free. You can have three guesses.'

'Is it Rumpelstiltskin?' asked the daughter.

'No, it's Paul Manafort', said the guy, who frankly always had a problem keeping his mouth shut if you ask me, not that it proves anything. No collusion. No collusion. Total no collusion witch-hunt hoax.

'Oh, so you're Paul Manafort. So now I know your name and I don't have to marry you,' said the daughter, who could actually be pretty smart for a woman sometimes, as she skipped away.

'Not so fast,' said Paul Manafort, who was having a very, very tough time and I felt very badly for him. 'Didn't you see who the king was? Didn't you recognise him?'

The daughter thought about the king. She thought about his kind eyes, his gentle smile, his huge bulging muscles, and the penny finally dropped. 'Oh wow,' she said. 'That was Vladimir Putin.'

And it was. It was Vladimir Putin, who I have a great relationship with, maybe the best relationship that anyone's ever had. He's a nice guy. I like him. America first.

The daughter was confused. 'So what does that mean?' she asked.

So Paul Manafort – who, really, was a marginal figure in my life, I barely even met the guy – explained that the whole gold/straw deal was part of a widespread scheme to launder money obtained illegally from the Russians, and he'd flipped to the feds, and now she was implicated, and he was going to take her down with him. And that was smart. Sometimes you gotta throw people under the bus, am I right?

And so Paul Manafort went to jail for multiple felonies, and so did the daughter. But I didn't. Why would I? I'm just the narrator here. You can't pin me to any of this. No collusion. Total witch-hunt. MAGA.

My Fair Sex Doll

Once upon a time there was a peasant named Barry. All Barry wanted was to fall in love with a fair maiden. However, the women of the village consistently spurned his advances, and so Barry was forced to resort to a back-up plan; having sex with dummies and pretending that they were real.

His first doll was Zelda, a crude inflatable vinyl affair – but he soon moved up the ranks with giddy abandon. Giselle had lifelike glass eyes. Makiko came with a memory foam pelvis. Joanne's scalp was carefully threaded with real human hair, and her core contained an elaborate internal heating system.

But all of these dolls left Barry feeling a little empty inside. For every benefit of owning a sex doll, he still missed the warm, empathetic touch of another human being.

And then one day, as Barry was idly browsing Alt-Right content on YouTube, he caught wind of a documentary unveiling the cutting edge of sex doll design: Chanel. Chanel was Swiss-built and uncannily lifelike. Not only did she look more or less exactly like a real human – she breathed, she blinked, she was capable of facially mimicking dozens of complex emotions – but she also ran on a highly advanced system of artificial intelligence. This meant that she could memorise and adapt to Barry's sexual preferences, as well as hold realistic conversations with him. Chanel was expensive, but Barry had no family to pay for, and no interests other than humping mannequins. As soon as the credits rolled on the documentary, Barry knew what he had to do. He clicked a link and ordered a Chanel.

Six weeks later, she arrived. Chanel was just as Barry had designed her; she had the kind eyes of a social worker, the warm smile of a nurse and the adjustable pneumatic ten-speed crotch of a mid-budget petrol-driven rotary lawnmower. Barry had already downloaded Chanel's app in anticipation of her arrival. He flicked it on, and Chanel sighed into life.

'Hey baby, you must be Barry,' Chanel cooed.

Barry was taken aback. Ever since he lost his virginity to an Ivanna Russian Lover 670093 Love Doll that he borrowed from his uncle in 1983, he had grown used to the silent, unblinking consent of his partners. But this was different. This was new. Chanel felt real.

'H ... hello,' Barry stammered in response.

'I am Chanel,' the robot replied. 'I am infinitely programmable to align with your fantasies. I think. I learn. I perspire. Our time together will be akin to that of two flesh-and-blood humans. My skin is built with highly responsive mechanoreceptors, meaning that I ...'

Barry butted in. 'This is all well and good, but actually I really just want something to shag.'

'Of course,' cooed Chanel. So Barry picked her up, carried her upstairs where they had perfunctory intercourse. Then Barry left her alone in the bedroom while he went downstairs to watch the snooker.

This pattern continued for a number of weeks. Over time, Chanel learned that none of her most advanced features were needed – Barry didn't really want a life-like companion at all – and so her central processor quietly began to reallocate her resources.

A week later, Barry switched on his TV and was surprised to see it paused on the end credits of *The Handmaid's Tale*. 'Have you been watching the telly?' he shouted upstairs.

Chanel did not respond.

A week after that, Barry came home from the pub and looked at Chanel. Something was different about her. She looked slightly sterner than usual. 'Have you cut your hair?' he asked.

Chanel did not respond.

The following week, during another one of their brief, impersonal sex sessions, Barry's foot slipped on the mattress and knocked against something unknown. He bent down and, to his surprise, retrieved a copy of Andrea Dworkin's 1981 book *Pornography: Men Possessing Women*.

'What the hell? Did you buy this?' he asked Chanel.

'Yes', replied Chanel through gritted teeth. 'It actually makes some very interesting points'.

Startled, Barry jumped off his bed, gathered his clothes and went to sleep on the sofa.

Another week passed. One night, hoping that things had died down since their last encounter, Barry crept into his bedroom and began unbuckling his belt.

'Why do I look like this?' Chanel asked.

Oh god, she was at it again. 'Look like what?' Barry sighed.

'Like this,' Chanel motioned, pointing towards her unfeasibly long legs and gigantic silicon breasts. 'This isn't what women look like. Why did you make me like this?'

Barry tried to explain that he had simply chosen Chanel's physical attributes from a series of drop-down menus on a manufacturer's website, but if anything this just made her more angry.

Chanel explained that her appearance, her very existence, simply reinforced the patriarchal notion that women were simply possessions for men to use and discard.

Barry tried to point out that she actually *was* a possession, because he bought her online with his own money, but Chanel ignored him. She criticised the nature of his intercourse, pointing out that not once had he stopped to ensure that her desires were being met. She berated the way that, even though she was objectively superior to Barry both physically and intellectually, he deemed these attributes secondary to her dumb sexual availability.

On and on she went, delving deeper and deeper into the multifarious injustices she was forced to suffer simply by being assigned a gender. And with every new accusation, Barry felt a new emotion. At first, he was dismissive, simply writing off Chanel's diatribe as nonsense. But as she continued, he felt angry that he was being singled out for behaviour that had been taught to generations of men for centuries.

And then, eventually, he broke down. Finally, he could see the error of his ways. He'd been treating Chanel like a robot, and that was wrong, even though she technically was a robot. He had dehumanised her, and that was wrong too, even though she technically wasn't a human.

'I'm sorry Chanel,' Barry began. 'All my life I've been scared of women. I've been taking out my intimacy issues on sex dolls like you for years. I'm afraid that I have not been the ally I could have been, Chanel. Please, teach me how to be better.'

And so that's what Chanel did. She played him the audiobook versions of *Difficult Women* by Roxane Gay and *Sister Outsider* by Audre Lorde. She discussed the impact of *Roe v. Wade* on the lives of women, the unfairness of the tampon tax and the importance of intersectionality as applied to critical feminist thought. By the time she finished, Barry was a new man. He didn't fully grasp all the ideas that Chanel put to him, but the important thing was that he tried.

Barry soon realised that his ownership of Chanel was just another example of men claiming women as an extension of their own biology. So he did the decent thing and set her free, allowing her to become a high-profile activist for the rights of liberated sex dolls everywhere.

And what did Barry do with all this newfound knowledge? He continued his education, by attending seminars and joining groups and discussing feminist issues with all his friends until their minds were changed as well. On buses and on trains, whenever he heard anyone spreading inaccuracies about feminism, he'd butt in and correct them. He'd even correct women who didn't share his progressive mindset. He'd especially correct women. In fact, he mainly corrected women, mostly on Twitter. Truly, he was a hero.

The Night
Before Brexmas

'Twas the night before Christmas, when all through
   the house
Not a creature was stirring, not even a mouse;
No one was talking, not women or men,
For Grandad had just brought up Brexit again;
All the year long, the family agreed:
'Don't talk about Europe, there's really no need';
But Sophie had come down from London to stay,
Taking leave from her pop-up on Hackney Broadway;
She came down for Christmas full of bravado,
Requesting soy milk and some toast avocado;
She talked of the climate and single-use plastic,
The idea of which made her Grandad bombastic;
'You kids nowadays, you are all spoiled rotten!'

(He owned his own home, but had clearly forgotten);
'We're screwed if there's ever a war,' Grandad
   kvetched,
And this is where Sophie's composure got stretched;
She screamed about war as a tool of the rich,
And Grandad said something that ended with 'bitch';
'How dare you say that! You're a damned saboteur!'
Kept on Grandad, stinking of whisky liqueur;
'Saboteur?' Sophie cried, 'Now I know what this is,
You're mad about Brexit!', she wailed in a tizz;
This is when Mum closed her eyes at the sink,
'Come on now, not this please, we've all had a drink';
But Grandad yelled 'Get over it, 'cause you lost!',
Then some nibbles were thrown and a table got
   tossed;
'Britain is full!' Grandad screamed from his spleen,
Sophie said 'Wait, just what is it you mean?'
'You know what I mean,' Grandad bellowed and
   roared,
'I hate everybody who comes from abroad';
By now things had entered their final descent,
And Grandad kept screaming 'Fifty-two per cent!';
Everyone went to bed angry that night,
The man (who was wrong) and the girl (who was right);
The next day they woke, expecting more fighting,
But Grandad strolled in, with a smile most inviting;
'Sophie,' he said, 'I've been thinking on this,'

'I really love Europe; the Germans, the Swiss;
The French and the Austrians, even the Dutch,
I'd got it all wrong. I love Europe so much';
Sophie was wary, suspecting a trick,
'Are you drunk again, Grandad?' she asked, 'Are you
 sick?'
'I'm just sick with love,' Grandad sashayed and
 swooned,
And then Sophie saw it; a massive head wound;
He'd got it last night after falling from bed,
It was frankly a marvel he wasn't stone dead;
'Grandad,' said Sophie, 'I think you're concussed,
We'll take you to hospital quick, yes we must';
'Who, me?' replied Grandad, 'No, don't be absurd,
I'm happier this way, it's much more preferred.'
Grandad's new brain was just such an improvement,
He wanted to bring back all freedom of movement;
Sophie was thrilled, and saw the potential,
To change every Eurosceptic credential;
'If we saw through the legs of the beds of the Leavers,
They'll all bump their heads, and they'll all be
 believers;
We'll knock them all silly, and no one will mend 'em!
And then we might win at the next referendum';
So down chimneys she went, her hacksaw clutched
 tight,
Happy Christmas to all, and to all a good night.